# Heading for t

## A fans' guide to rugby

**Michael Miles**

**London League Publications Ltd**

**Heading for the line**
A fans' guide to rugby league grounds



Front cover: Heading to Wembley on Challenge Cup Final day 2012; Hemel Stags versus London Broncos Under-19s, January 2013. Back cover: The terracing at Odsal, January 2013; A London bus and Wembley on Challenge Cup Final day 2012.



A CIP catalogue record for this book is available from the British Library.

First published in Great Britain in April 2013 by:
London League Publications Ltd, P.O. Box 65784, London NW2 9NS

ISBN: 978-1903659- 67-0

Cover design by: Stephen McCarthy Graphic Design
46, Clarence Road, London N15 5BB

Layout: Peter Lush

Printed and bound in Great Britain by Charlesworth Press, Wakefield

# Foreword: Rugby League grounds

Oh the grounds of my youth, when we travelled all over the north of England by train or in a tiny, 32-seater bus ('charabanc', to be precise) to watch rugby league. And was there any ground ever, anywhere, like the now defunct Belle Vue Rangers venue in Manchester where, in one day, we could watch St Helens play Belle Vue, ride on the funfair, visit the zoo and take in the excitement of the speedway at night? Truly it was the Disneyland of the 1940s and the early 1950s for the 13-a-side code's devotees. What of Station Road, the home of the once mighty Swinton? As its name implied, 'away' spectators invariably arrived by train and alighted at the railway station which virtually adjoined the once 30,000 plus stadium. And we youngsters could collect train numbers for at least half an hour before and after kick off!

Watersheddings, once home to the Oldham club, had a greyhound racing track alongside its pitch. But it was so cold, even in August when, as a player, I was forced to sit and rest under the main grandstand at half-time rather than trek back to the distant and antiquated changing rooms. Salford possessed changing rooms at its old and famous Willows ground which had such low ceilings, supported by iron girders, that I have even seen players injured before taking to the pitch and, having banged their heads on such hazards, emerge from the tunnel swathed in bandages.

What, too, of the 'Pigeon Loft' at Bramley's Barley Mow ground where the teams changed in a wooden loft-like construction (adjoining the Barley Mow pub) and had to enter the field by overcoming a steep set of descending wooden steps.

Every ground was unique to each club and, apart from an occasional portakabin bar and cafeteria on the terracing, there was little to comfort the spectators other than the 80 minutes of rugby itself.

Today, the modern stadia of the vast majority of our Super League clubs are the town's or city's equivalent of the coliseums which our friends the ancient Romans built in their major cities to provide entertainment and income for all. Such stadiums as at St Helens, Wigan, Hull, Salford and elsewhere, though lacking the individuality of those of yesteryear, are designed with spectator comfort and entertainment in mind with their many restaurants, bars, lounges, meeting rooms and even crèches for before, during and after the matches. Such grounds have become the focal point of the town or city, and day and night they now cater for any social, business, or sporting events required by the local population. Gate money at the matches, though a priority, is now no longer the sole income of any ambitious club for the revenue streams created by having a 24 hours a day use of the stadium is vital to the success of any club. Whether wining, dining, or simply watching rugby league, supporters now expect not just a game, but an experience when they visit their local ground.

Many wander around the concourse at Saints' new Langtree Park to view the giant murals depicting the club's former great players. At the Halliwell Jones Stadium, Warrington Wolves' fans can, on occasions, browse around their concourse amid market stalls, while at the Stobart Stadium in Widnes, a museum highlighting the history of the Vikings is available for all.

Yes, at our local rugby league grounds, as the song suggests, "the times, they are a' changing".

**Ray French MBE**

Ray French had a distinguished career in both rugby codes, and was a dual-code international. He is also a distinguished writer and journalist on both codes of rugby, and for many years was the BBC Television rugby league commentator. He has made an enormous contribution to the game, and has also always been very supportive of London League Publications Ltd.

## How to use this book:

We have done our best to make this book up to date. If while visiting a ground you find out of date information, please let us know so we can amend future editions, either email: peter@llpshop.co.uk or by post: PO Box 65784, London NW2 9NS

**Road travel:** We have included local landmarks, but they may change (i.e. a particular shop close). If not using sat nav we would recommend a standard road map.

**Facilities:** Not all stands are open and all facilities available all the time. If a particular facility is important to you, check in advance. Prices are for 2013 season unless otherwise stated.

The three clubs new to the professional game are all developing facilities at their grounds, information in this book is as at the start of the 2013 season.

**Transport:** Services vary, especially on Sundays; always check in advance.

**Facilities for supporters with disabilities:** We would advise always phone the club you are visiting in advance, and book the facilities you require.

Please note that the authors, and London League Publications Ltd, do not accept any liability for any loss, injury or inconvenience sustained by people as a result of using the information or advice in this book.

# Introduction

My earliest memories of rugby league are of watching it on BBC TV's *Grandstand* on Saturday afternoons while listening to the unmistakeable Eddie Waring.

I was living in Hereford – hardly a rugby league hotbed – but now, living in London, I was curious when a couple of years ago the *Evening Standard* ran a promotion offering free tickets to watch Harlequins Rugby League as they were then called.

It was summer, the game was just four miles down the A316 at the Twickenham Stoop, and I was beginning to suffer live-sport deficiency so I went along. And it was a thoroughly enjoyable experience.

I ought to make a small confession here. I have always been more of a football fan. I support West Ham United and the likes of Chelsea, Fulham and QPR are within easy reach of my West London home. But I was beginning to tire of the inevitable hype surrounding Premiership football, not to mention the soaring cost of everything from admission to programmes. It was a pleasant surprise to spend a sunny summer Saturday sitting where I wanted among fans who were there to enjoy the game and not start World War III.

I went to the Stoop another half-a dozen times that season, and while I would not pretend even now to understand all that is going on (could someone explain the offside law?) I thoroughly enjoyed the experience.

I also love sports stadiums. To quote the rugby (union) writer Stephen Jones in his book *Midnight Rugby:* "Each of the arenas where rugby is played is emphatically different; each has its own appearance, atmosphere and facilities, its own concept of design... bunged together bit by bit as each wedge of cash has become available."

I write this at the start of a year when the Rugby League World Cup will be played in this country, and with it an opportunity to attract fans like me to this great sport. So the aim of this book is simple. It is to provide the travelling rugby league fan access to all the information they need to get the maximum out of their rugby travels.

Supporters are the lifeblood of the game. But with the increasingly odd times and dates for games, life is much easier for the armchair supporter than those who trail to distant towns for a Sunday kick-off during a March blizzard.

I hope you find it useful, and the book enhances your enjoyment of rugby league.

**Michael Miles**
**Chiswick, March 2013**

Michael Miles is 61 years old, married with 2 'grown-up' children and lives in West London and somehow ended up supporting West Ham United and the London Broncos. He loves watching live sport, and is fortunate in having a number of premier league football and rugby union clubs close at hand.

He says: "Alas, there is only one first class rugby league team nearby and it is doubly unfortunate that it happens to be the London Broncos, one of the worst teams in Super League over recent seasons. But let it not be said I let a poor team get in the way of my sporting enjoyment."

Most of his working life was spent in the circulation departments of consumer magazines, although in recent years he managed to find the time to contribute to a number of rugby and football publications (*Rugby World, The Rugby Paper, Late Tackle*), as well as writing regular match reports for the website *The Ball is Oval.*

## Bibliography

**Websites:** The first port of call is always the club's own website, though these vary enormously in both the quantity and quality of information, particularly when it comes to keeping them updated.

Often maligned, but not to be ignored, is Wikipedia, especially when it comes to quirky information about stadia. The following were also helpful:
www.therfl.co.uk: The Rugby Football League's own website
www.loverugbyleague.com: Reasonable coverage of most Super-League and Championship clubs.
www.rugbyleaguechampionships.co.uk: "new-look" site for the Championship.
http://nationalconferenceleague.co.uk: Site for all Conference clubs.
www.levelplayingfield.org.uk: Site for the charity that looks after the interests of disabled supporters.

**Books:** Not a lot to choose from, though I would heartily recommend *The Grounds of Rugby League* by Trevor Delaney. Published in 1991, it is out of date, but offers a wonderful flavour of the game and grounds in the pre summer rugby era. The *Gillette Rugby League Yearbook*, while concerning itself less with what is off the pitch, is nevertheless a reminder that what still matters most is what takes place on the pitch. Honourable mention must also be made of *A Fan's Guide: The Football Grounds of England and Wales* by Duncan Adams. Very useful where grounds are shared.

**Magazines:** *Rugby League World* and its weekly sister *League Express* kept me up to date. Of particular interest and relevance was the 'Secret Speccie' feature in *Rugby League World.*

# Contents

Sign of the times: Advert on Iffley Road, Oxford, for the home team's first rugby league match at this historic rugby union ground, 13 April 2013.

Oxford versus South Wales Scorpions, 13 April 2013. The first home match for the Oxford team.

One of the stands at Iffley Road, home of Oxford University RFC, and the new Oxford rugby league team.

# 1. British professional clubs

## Barrow Raiders

**Ground:** Craven Park
**Address:** Duke Street, Barrow-in-Furness, LA14 1XP
**Phone:** 01229 830470 (stadium office)
**Website:** www.barrowrlfc.com
**E-mail:** info@barrowrlfc.com
**Colours:** Blue and White
**Capacity:** 7,600.

**Stadium history:** Barrow joined the Northern Union in 1897. Craven Park was built in 1931, largely through the efforts of the club's supporters, 500 of whom volunteered to construct the ground. The cost of the building project was £7,500. The stadium is named after Commander G. W. Craven, a local war hero, who had started the appeal fund with a £500 donation. Look out for the Willie Horne statue near the stadium. The ground has one stand, two covered terraces and one open terrace, with some terracing by the stand.

**Ticket prices:** adult: £15; concessions: £10; under-16: £5; under-five free. Transfer to grandstand £1. Family tickets £30 (two adults, up to three children) available from 78, Scott St in advance, not on day of the game.

**Supporters with disabilities:** Wheelchair access is available at the main gate. Disabled toilets are in the Willie Horne Stand next to the players' tunnel. All 12 accessible spaces are under cover in the Willie Horne Stand.

**Club shop:** 78 Scott Street, Barrow LA14 1QE. Open Monday to Wednesday 9am to 4pm, Thursday and Friday: 9am to 3.45pm, Saturday: 10am to midday. Phone: 01229 820273. Shop at ground near Willie Horne Stand.

**Refreshments:** Raiders Bar on match days. There is also a catering stall.

**Directions:**

**Rail:** Barrow in Furness station is around three-quarters of a mile from the ground. Turn right on Hibbert Road, then right into Abbey Road. At roundabout by Barrow Library, turn right into Duke Street, left into Willie Horne Way, then left into Clive Street.

**Road:** From M6, junction 36 for 'Barrow and Lake district'. Follow signs for Barrow-in-Furness on A590 into Barrow-in-Furness, heading for Walney Island and Barrow Town centre. This road is Hindpool Road. After the Lidl Supermarket on the left-hand side, take the next left into Duke Street. Continue for approximately 500 yards, Craven Park is on the right.

**Parking:** There is no parking at the ground. There is ample on-street parking next to the ground, plus other local parking. People can be dropped off at the entrance to the ground (Willie Horne Way or Hindpool Road end).

# Batley Bulldogs

**Ground:** Mount Pleasant
**Address:** Heritage Way, Batley WF17 7NZ
**Phone:** 01924 470 062
**Fax:** 01924 470 062
**Website:** www.batleybulldogs.co.uk
**E-mail:** info@batleybulldogs.co.uk
**Colours:** Purple
**Capacity:** 7,200.

**About the Stadium:** Batley were one of the 22 clubs that formed the Northern Union in 1895. They have always played at Mount Pleasant, which adjoins a cricket ground. The ground has undergone a modernisation programme in recent years, with a new stand and covered terrace. Renowned for its famous slope, Mount Pleasant is at the top of the hill that overlooks Batley. The end of the ground at the top of the hill is surrounded by three grandstands. Behind the posts is a relatively new covered terrace, which also has the directors' rooms and executive boxes. At the opposite end of the hill is an open terrace. Along one of the sides there is a modern covered seated stand and a terrace is closed off for safety reasons. On the far side is a covered stand. The bottom corner of the pitch sees quite a large dip, which the home side use to their advantage.
**Ticket prices:** adult: £15; concession: £10; kids: £3.

**Supporters with disabilities:** Contact Andrew Winner on 01924 470062. There are 12 accessible car parking spaces on a first-come, first-served basis. There are 40 accessible seats for home and away supporters on a first-come, first-served basis. There are accessible toilets and catering facilities near the entrance to the ground.

**Refreshments:** Refreshment kiosks behind the main stand. There is also food and drink in the north-west corner of the ground.

**Directions:**

**Rail:** Batley station is about one mile away. Go along Back Station Road to Station Road, then turn right onto Rouse Mill Lane. Turn left onto Bradford Road (A652) and then right onto Taylor Street. At end turn left onto Purlwell Hall Road and left into Heritage Road which leads to the ground.

**Buses:** www.wymetro.com

**Road:** Leave the M62 at Junction 26 and follow signs for the A638. Follow through Cleckheaton Town Centre and turn right after Fox's Biscuits up to the top of the hill. Then turn left into Heritage Road.

**Parking:** Club car parks, and at side of the ground. Also side streets.

# Bradford Bulls

**Ground:** Odsal Stadium
**Address:** Odsal, Bradford, West Yorkshire BD6 1BS
**Phone:** 08448 711 491
**Website:** www.bradfordbulls.co.uk
**E-mail:** info@bradfordbulls.co.uk
**Twitter:** @OfficialBullsRL
**Colours:** White, with black, red and yellow facings
**Capacity:** 27,491. **Seats:** 5,850. **Standing:** 21,641.

**Club history:** The original Bradford Football Club was formed in 1863, and played rugby football, subsequently joining the Rugby Football Union. Bradford was among the 22 clubs who seceded from the RFU in 1895 to form the Northern Union. Bradford was formed as Bradford Northern in 1907, after a split from Bradford Park Avenue, which switched to played Association Football. The club was renamed Bradford Bulls in 1996 at the start of Super League.

**Stadium history:** Before moving to Odsal Northern had two other homes at Greenfield Athletic Ground in Dudley Hill and at Birch Lane. On June 20 1933 Bradford Northern signed a 10-year lease with Bradford council for a former quarry being used as a waste dump at Odsal Top, and turned it into the biggest stadium outside Wembley. Bradford Northern played their first match there on 1 September 1934. In 1952 Bradford beat New Zealand in the first floodlit football match of any code in the north of England.
In 1953, Northern's highest ever attendance of 69,429 watched Bradford play Huddersfield in the Challenge Cup third round.
By 1963 Bradford Northern's support had declined so rapidly that only 324 saw them play Barrow, and the club went out of business on 10 December 1963. In July 1964 Bradford Northern (1964) Ltd came into existence. 14,500 spectators turned out to see the reformed club play Hull KR.

**The Stadium:** There are three areas of the Stadium: Tetley's main stand, the Coral Stand and terracing. The Tetley's main stand provides seats under cover. The Coral Stand has executive boxes and function suites.
The remainder of the stadium is terracing. There is no segregation at Odsal, but away fans generally are on the terraces behind the posts. The home fans are situated at either side of the ground, with the corporate facilities behind the goal. Check the weather forecast, the terracing is uncovered, although there are plans to provide cover for the main terrace.
There are facilities for hire for conferences, weddings, etc. Contact the club for details.
The stadium, apart from the Coral Stand, is in urgent need of modernisation. It's great on a warm summer day with a big crowd, but can be cold and bleak otherwise.

**Ticket office:** Tickets available either at turnstiles or ticket office on game days, or to pre-purchase call the ticket office on 08448 711 490. Credit card purchases can be made at the ticket office.

**Ticket Prices: Premier club:** adult: £30; concession: £25; student: £25; under-16s: £25.
**Main stand:** adults £25; concession £20; student: £20; junior (12 to 15): £15; under-12: free;
**Terrace:** adults £20; concession £15; student: £15; junior (12 to 15): £10; Under-12s: free.
Children under 12 are admitted free if accompanied by an adult.

**Supporters with disabilities:** There are 50 car park spaces. Vouchers are allocated to those with a blue parking badge. There are 33 spaces for home wheelchair users and six for away supporters. They are at the rear of the hospitality stand. Ring the ticket office on 0448 711 490 to discuss options. There are accessible toilets in the terracing, at the back of the main stand and in the hospitality stand. Seats for ambulant disabled in the main stand.

**Club shop:** Bradford Bulls Merchandise Store, Odsal Stadium, Odsal Bradford BD6 1BS. 08448 711 490. Open on match days – contact club for other opening times. www.bradfordbulls.co.uk/shop

**Refreshments:** Refreshment vans are located in both the terracing and at the back of the main stand. Three brand new bar facilities have been constructed on the middle concourse around the stadium. These will be licensed serving both alcoholic and non-alcoholic drinks.
The Touchdown has also been converted into a public bar, as has the Pavilion Bar located behind the Tetley's Stand
Outside the ground, the Odsal Top is across the road from the ground.

**Directions:**

**Air:** Bradford has its own international airport, with regular flights from the major destinations in the UK and Europe. The airport is located to the North-east of the city, approximately 11 miles from the Odsal stadium by road.

**Rail:** Bradford Interchange is situated in the heart of Bradford, and connects the main Trans-Pennine route between Manchester and Leeds with local trains and bus services. Leeds Station is serviced by GNER, Arriva Trains Northern, Midland Mainline and Virgin Trains.

**Buses:** The major bus provider in the city is First Bradford. From Bradford Interchange, First Bradford services 508, 614 (eastbound carriageway only) and 624 (westbound carriageway only) pass by the stadium. Many services go down Manchester Road, which is a short walk from the stadium. Get off at the Richard Dunn Sports complex.
www.firstgroup.com/ukbus/yorkhumber/bradford/home

**Road:**

**From M62 motorway (East, West & South):**
From the M62, take junction 26, follow the signs for the M606. Take the M606 and come off at Junction 1.
Take the second exit left on to A6038 (Rooley Avenue) and follow the road to first roundabout. At roundabout turn left and after 50 yards take first left into Stadium Road. The Stadium is located at the end of the road.
**From Bradford City centre & Interchange:** Follow the signs for the A641, and join it, Manchester Road. After approximately four miles from the City centre take the exit signposted Odsal and continue up the slip road to the roundabout. At the roundabout take the second exit and proceed for 50 yards before taking the first left into Stadium Road. The Stadium is situated at the end of the road.

**Parking at ground:** Game day parking for pass holders is available in the Stadium Car Parks A-E, accessible via Stadium Road. Parking for non-pass holders is available in the Richard Dunn Car Park, located directly opposite the Stadium on the A6038 (Rooley Avenue). Cost: £4 a car.

**Parking nearby:** Free, unsecure parking on the road at Slaithgate Lane. Exit M606 at Junction 2 and turn left, then immediately right onto Slaithgate Lane. The best place is opposite the older industrial units on the right hand side of the road, just before the roundabout for Junction 3 of the M606.

## Castleford Tigers

**Ground:** The Wish Communications Stadium
**Address:** Wheldon Road, Castleford, WF10 2SD
**Phone:** 01977 552674
**Fax:** 01977 518007
**Website:** www.castigers.com
**E-mail:** info@castigers.com
**Twitter:** @CTRLFC
**Colours:** Black and amber
**Capacity:** 12,000. **Seats:** 1,500. **Standing:** 10,500

**Stadium history:** Castleford Tigers was formed in 1926, and has played their home games at Wheldon Road since 1927. There have been plans for some time for the Tigers to move to a new site at Glasshoughton. However, it now (October 2012) seems possible that they will try to redevelop their current ground to bring it up to a modern standard.

**The stadium:** The Tigers play their home games at The Wish Communications Stadium. The ground was previously named 'The Jungle' after an earlier sponsorship. Before that it was named after the road in which it is situated, 'Wheldon Road'.
Despite its lack of modernisation the ground is believed to offer one of the best and most volatile atmospheres in the game. The ground has covered seating and uncovered terracing on one side, with covered standing down the full length of the other side. Both ends are standing, again with one covered (generally home fans) and one open. The away fans usually congregate in the open end, although some like to stand in the covered terrace at the side. The terracing itself is steep, and the stands are close to the pitch, so the view is all right and the atmosphere is good.
To be brutal, the ground is well past its best and is from an earlier time in sports stadiums. That's what happens when a club waits for years expecting their home to be bulldozed. It's essentially the stadium built in 1935 and improved in the late 1960s, and now held together by layers of black and gold paint. It's a relic, but not without charm.

**Ticket office:** Online: www.castigers.com/tickets
Phone: 01977 555 336, 9.30am to 5.30 pm Monday to Saturday, Sunday 10am to 4pm.
In person: Club shop in Carlton Lanes Shopping Centre
Open: 9.30am to 5.30 pm Monday to Friday; Saturday 9am to 5pm.

**Ticket prices: Standing:** adults £19; senior citizens, students, juniors: £11.
**Seating:** Adults £22; senior citizens, students, juniors £14. Reductions for tickets bought in advance.

Pre-purchased standing tickets can be transferred to the main stand (seating) on the day for an extra £3.

**Supporters with disabilities:** Contact: Jessica Dovey on 01977 552674. There are 27 accessible parking spaces, and parking is allocated on a first-come, first-served booking system, and supporters are advised to book a space the week before the game.
Accessible seating is found at the front of the main stand for both home and away supporters. There are 14 accessible spaces for home fans and six for away supporters.
An accessible toilet is located 30 metres from the accessible seating.

**Club shop:** Tigers Den, Carlton Lanes Shopping centre, Castleford, WF10 1AD. Phone: 01977 555 336. There is also a shop at the ground. Online orders via the club's website.

**Refreshments:** Wheldon Road has several fast-food outlets in the ground serving food ranging from burgers to hot-dogs, chips and chocolate bars. Drinks are generally soft bottled drinks, tea or coffee, although beer is available from the tent outside the main stand.
The Tigers restaurant offers a three course pre-match meal, and hospitality packages are available.

**Local refreshments:** Wheldon Road features plenty of pubs for a pre-match drink. The Boot Room, situated directly outside the ground, is the main pub where both home and away fans congregate.
Nearer to Castleford town centre are The Garden House and The Early Bath pubs. The Early Bath is a shrine to Castleford and Rugby league. There are memorabilia from most clubs covering every inch of wall and ceiling.
The Magnet pub on Pontefract Road, if coming from the M62, Junction 32, provides good food, although this has to be booked in advance.

**Directions:**

**Rail:** Regular trains run from both Leeds and Sheffield to Castleford. However, with games usually played on a Sunday, services may be affected by track maintenance. The station is in the centre of town and is a 15 minute walk from the ground. From Powell Street, turn right into Carlton Street and at roundabout, cross Bridge Street into Wheldon Road.

**Bus:** The bus station is in the centre of Castleford, and from there it's a 15 minute walk to the ground. Walk towards Wood Street, turn up Albion St (pass café and health centre), turn right into Carlton Street then as for train station.

**Road:**

**From East:** Leave the M62 at junction 32. At roundabout take the third exit onto the A639 (signposted Castleford). At traffic signals continue onto

the A656. Continue on the A656, go over three roundabouts, and at the fourth roundabout take the 3rd exit onto Wheldon road.
**From South/North:** Leave the A1 (M) at junction 41, then join the M62 motorway. Leave the M62 at junction 32. At roundabout take the third exit onto the A639 (sign posted Castleford). At traffic signals continue onto the A656. Continue on the A656, go over three roundabouts, and at the fourth roundabout take the 3rd exit onto Wheldon road.
**From West:** Leave the M62 at junction 31. At roundabout take the second exit onto the A655, signposted Castleford. Continue on the A655, go through three roundabouts, and at the fourth roundabout take the second exit onto Wheldon Road.

**Parking:** The club opens the training field adjacent to the ground on match-days, and there is also ample side-street parking.
There is also limited parking in Carlton Lanes Shopping Centre car park. Castlefield's car park behind Carlton Lanes has free parking on a Sunday and there are plenty of spaces.

## Dewsbury Rams

**Ground:** The Tetley's Stadium
**Address** Owl Lane, Dewsbury, West Yorkshire WF12 7RH
**Phone:** 01924 465 489
**Fax:** 01924 437 201
**Website:** www.dewsburyrams.co.uk
**E-mail:** info@dewsburyrams.co.uk
**Twitter:** @DewsburyRams
**Colours:** Red, amber and black
**Capacity:** 3,500; **seats:** 900; **standing:** 2,600

**Stadium history:** Dewsbury joined the Northern Union in 1898. They are most famous for becoming champions in 1972–73 after finishing the regular season in 8th place. In the play-offs they beat Featherstone Rovers and Warrington away, and then Leeds in the Championship Final.
Crown Flatt, known as the Tetley's Stadium for sponsorship reasons, is on the site of Shaw Cross Colliery, which closed in August 1968. Crown Flatt was also the name of a stadium used by Dewsbury until 13 September 1988, when it was burnt down in an arson attack.

**The stadium:** Built in 1994, the Tetley's Stadium is relatively new. There are two stands, one seated (North) and one standing (South), and ample space on the grass bankings behind both goals.
The home fans tend to congregate in the centre of both stands, although, when the weather is fine, the grass bankings are a popular spot for families. With two open ends, the ground is wide open to the elements. More often than not, a strong wind whistles through the stadium, so visiting fans are advised to take an extra layer, just in case!

**Ticket prices: North stand (seats):** adult: £15; over 60s and students: £9; under-16s: £9. **South stand (standing):** adult: £13; over 60s and students: £7; under-16s: £2.

**Supporters with disabilities:** There are nine accessible parking spaces (three for away supporters) in front of the main entrance, Unlimited parking behind South Stand on a first-come, first-served basis.
There are six accessible spaces for home supporters and six for away supporters, all under cover.
All boxes and hospitality areas are accessible as well as catering facilities and toilets.

**Club shop:** The club shop is at the rear of the North Stand and is open on match-days for one hour prior to kick-off, and for 30 minutes after the match. Online: http://dewsbury.rlstore.co.uk or via club website.

**Refreshments:** The Bailey Bar is located on the North Stand ground floor and is open two hours prior to kick-off. The Royal Suite on the North Stand first floor usually opens 90 minutes before kick-off and remains open throughout and after the match.
The South Stand bar at the rear of the South Stand opens 90 minutes before kick-off and closes at the end of half-time.

**Directions:**

**Rail:** From Dewsbury railway station a taxi to the stadium will cost £3 to £4. The station is around 2.5 miles from the ground.

**Bus:** The bus station is on Aldams Road about a five minute walk from the railway station. From the railway station cross the road, go down Wellington Road, left into Wellington Street, right into Old Westgate, left into Southgate and left onto South Street. The bus station is on the right. Buses 202 and 203 in the Leeds direction go near the ground in about 12 minutes. The fare is £1.30 (2012).

**Road:**

**From M62:** Leave the M62 at Junction 28 and follow the signs for Dewsbury (A653). Just after the petrol station on the left the dual carriageway will merge into one lane and back into two as it comes to traffic lights.
Be in the left hand lane. Turn left at the lights and follow the road round to the roundabout. Turn left at the roundabout and the stadium is on the right.

**From M1:** Leave the M1 at Junction 40 and follow the signs to Dewsbury. This is the A638 dual carriageway. At the end of the dual carriageway turn right at the roundabout onto Owl Lane. The Tetley's Stadium is on the left hand side.

**Parking:** Car parking in the main car park behind the South Stand is £2 per vehicle. There is also limited room on the roads near the industrial estate 500 metres to the north of the stadium. However, there is usually ample parking at the ground.

# Doncaster

**Ground:** Keepmoat Stadium
**Address:** Stadium Way, Lakeside, Doncaster, South Yorkshire, DN4 5JW
**Phone:** 01302 765 888
**Fax:** 01302 321 961
**Website:** www.doncasterrugbyleague.co.uk
**E-mail:** carlhall@doncasterrlfc.co.uk
**Twitter:** @doncaster_rlfc
**Colours:** Blue/Gold
**Capacity:** 15,231 (all seated)

**Stadium history:** Keepmoat Stadium is a multi-purpose stadium. It cost approximately £32million to build, and as well as Doncaster RLFC, is used by Doncaster Rovers Football Club. The first sporting fixture was between Doncaster RLFC and Sheffield Eagles on 27 December 2006. The stadium is sponsored under a long-term contract by Keepmoat, a company specialising in social housing. There are other sporting facilities at the stadium.

**The stadium:** On one side is the West stand, which is the main stand, containing the dressing rooms. Opposite is the Doncaster Success Stand. Both ends of the ground are identical. The stadium is situated next to a lake, which must make it unique.

**Ticket office:** 01302 762 576
**Ticket prices:** adult: £15; concessions: £12; junior (5 to 16): £3; under-5s: free.

**Supporters with disabilities:** Contact: Roy Green on 01302 765888 or 07506 647 571. There are 120 accessible car parking spaces 25 metres away. There are 61 accessible seats for both home and away supporters, 54 in the East Stand and seven on the balcony. There are accessible catering and toilet facilities nearby. The 16 boxes all have disabled access. The club has an induction loop. Assistance dogs are welcome.

**Club shop:** Phone: 01302 765 888. Items are on sale at the stadium on matchdays.

**Refreshments:** The food inside is the usual fare, and the concourses are quite spacious. There are hospitality packages available, linked to hiring a box for the day.

**Local refreshments:** As the stadium is on the outskirts of town, there is not much choice in the way of pubs.
There is The Lakeside, a Beefeater outlet near Stadium Way (visible to the right of it if driving towards the stadium from Junction 3 of the M18). There is a bar in the bowling alley next to the Vue Cinema, which is situated on the other side of the lake.

**Directions**

**Air:** Robin Hood (Doncaster / Sheffield) Airport is eight miles from the stadium.
**Rail:** Doncaster station is just under two miles away so it is probably wise to take a taxi to the ground. For the 25 to 30 minute walk, coming out of the station turn right and keep straight on this road (A6182 Trafford Way), and eventually reach the stadium complex on the left.
Alternatively, there is access to the stadium by bus from Frenchgate Interchange, which is next door to the train station.

**Bus:** First Bus 72 & 75 services will operate from the Doncaster Frenchgate Interchange every 20 minutes between 5.30am and 6pm, Monday to Saturday, then hourly thereafter until 9.15pm, and every 30 minutes between 9.35am and 6.05pm on Sundays.
An enhanced bus service operates on match days. These start and terminate at the Frenchgate bus station.

**Road:** From the A1 (M) join the M18 eastbound at junction 35 (signposted Hull), or from the M1, join the M18 eastbound at junction 32. Once on the M18, leave at junction 3 and take the A6182 towards Doncaster (the stadium is well signposted from junction 3 and is about 1.5 miles away). Pass a retail park on the left and then at the next island (which has the Lakeside pub visible behind it) turn left onto White Rose Way. The Lakeside Shopping Centre is now on the right (the stadium is located directly behind the shopping centre). At the next island turn right onto the industrial estate and after passing the Tesco distribution centre on the right, turn right at the bottom of the road and the stadium is further down on the left.

**Parking at ground:** There are 1,000 car parking spaces at the stadium. The cost is £5 a car.

**Parking nearby:** A number of firms on the nearby industrial park offer matchday parking at around £3 to £4 a vehicle. There is some free street parking.

# Featherstone Rovers

**Ground:** Big Fellas Stadium
**Address:** Post Office Road, Featherstone, WF7 5EN
**Phone:** 01977 702 386
**Fax:** 01977 602 675
**Website:** www.featherstonerovers.net
**E-mail:** info@featherstonerovers.net
**Colours:** Navy Blue/White
**Capacity:** 6,750; **Seats:** 3,700; **Standing:** 3,050.

**Stadium history:** Rovers are one of the 'small town' teams that were an important part of the development of the sport. Featherstone is a former coalmining town with a population of around 16,000. To many people they are known as Fev or The Colliers, highlighting the close link between the club and the local mining community. The club has a reputation for producing a conveyor belt of talented players and has enjoyed considerable success over the years.
The ground opened in 1904 and has been used by the club since their formation in 1908. From 2007, the ground was renamed the Chris Moyles stadium after the Radio 1 disc jockey. This attracted criticism from fans who felt Moyles had nothing to do with the club, or even rugby league. He was born in Leeds and is a well-known Leeds United fan. Moyles did not pay any money, but did occasionally mention Featherstone Rovers on his radio show. From 2009 the ground was sponsored by the Big Fellas nightclub.

**The stadium:** Post Office Road has a clubhouse and stand alongside one side of the pitch; on the opposite side is an all-seat stand with a roof. The two ends are terracing, where away fans are often found.
West terrace, main stand and clubhouse: built 1987; capacity 1,300; seats 950. Railway End (North): built 1980; capacity: 900; seats: none. East terrace and SCS Components Community Stand: built 1997; capacity 3,550; seats 2,750. Post Office Road end: built 1980: capacity 900; seats: none.
The future may see further development around Post Office Road. The club owns an expanse of land around the current stadium and there are plans for a supermarket, community sports facility, and a purpose-built 12,000 capacity stadium, though this could be reduced to a 6,500 modular design. It depends on a successful bid for Super League membership in 2015 or 2018. At the time of writing work is ongoing to further develop the Railway End.

**Ticket prices:** adult: £17; senior and concessions: £10; child: £5.

**Supporters with disabilities:** Contact: Paul Fowler on 07947 369336 or email: fowlerp53@sky.com

There are eight parking spaces in the main car park, by the turnstiles, and behind the Family Stand, next to the turnstile. There are 28 accessible seats shared between home and away supporters, 16 in the Community Stand, and 12 in the Main Stand. There is an accessible toilet in the Community Stand and one in the main stand.

**Club shop:** http://feathers.rlstore.co.uk . There is a shop at the ground which is open on match days and during the week.

**Refreshments:** The Atrium is the main clubhouse bar, and is open from 12.30pm on afternoon match-days. The Blue Lagoon is under the SCS Components Community Stand and offers a full range of cold drinks. The Rovers Pie Hut is in the Post Office Road Terrace, and sells pies, hot dogs and snacks. Next door is a bar selling canned alcoholic drinks. At the rear of the main stand is the Rovers Café Bar, offering hot and cold food and drinks. There are also pubs near the ground.

**Directions:**

**Rail:** Featherstone railway station is approximately three minutes walk from the ground. Go down station Lane and turn into Post Office Road.

**Road:** Leave the M62 at Junction 31 and follow the A645. Then turn left on to Station Lane.

**Parking at ground:** There is a small club car park primarily for home fans, but there are plenty of side streets near to the ground.

# Gateshead Thunder

**Ground:** Gateshead International Stadium (The Thunderdome)
**Address:** Neilson Road, Gateshead, Tyne & Wear NE10 0EF
**Phone:** 01914 335 710
**Fax:** 01914 335 706
**Website:** www.thunderrugby.com
**E-mail:** info@thunderrugby.com
**Twitter:** @thunderrugby
**Colours:** Blue
**Capacity:** 11,800 (All-Seated)

**Stadium history:** Gateshead Thunder was founded in 1999, and is the only professional rugby league club in the North-East of England. It was awarded a rugby league franchise after a three-way contest with Cardiff and Swansea. But Super League participation lasted only one season, and the franchise moved to Hull.
Since the demise of the original Thunder side, the club has struggled to survive. Relations with the stadium have been strained at times, with a possible move to Newcastle Falcon's Kingston Park mooted, but in 2008 the club committed itself to Gateshead Stadium for the immediate future.
The original stadium was built in 1955 at a cost of £30,000 and was known as the Gateshead Youth Stadium. At the turn of the 1970s Gateshead Council, the owners of the stadium, decided to invest heavily in it in an attempt to regenerate east Gateshead. Although the stadium caters primarily for athletics, it is also home to Gateshead Thunder and Gateshead FC, who play in the Blue Square Conference.

**The stadium:** Gateshead International Stadium and its various facilities occupy about 60 acres of land. The main arena is an all-seater, bowl-shape, consisting of four stands of red seats.
The main stand is the Tyne and Wear Stand, a steep, cantilevered structure which opened in 1981 and seats 3,300 spectators. Opposite is the East Stand, a 4,000-seat capacity structure which had been uncovered until 2010 when a cantilevered canopy roof was installed.
This is primarily an athletics stadium, so fans are quite a distance from the pitch. Seats are unreserved and the fans generally mix.
Occasionally matches are played at other venues, so check in advance.

**Ticket prices:** Adults: £10; concessions £5.

**Supporters with disabilities:** There are eight accessible parking spaces 30 metres from the stadium, shared between home and away supporters. There are 16 accessible seats, all under cover. Gateshead Council has an induction loop facility available. Contact: Claire White on 0191 433 5710 or 07854 965 409.

**Club Shop:** phone: 0191 433 5716.
http://thunderrugby.wix.com/thundershop

**Refreshments:** Enter the ground near the main reception. There is a small room with a merchandise desk, and then a canteen style bar that sells food and drink. There are the usual pies, hot dogs, alcoholic and non-alcoholic drinks available inside the ground. Hospitality packages available.

**Directions:**

**Air:** Newcastle International Airport is seven miles to the north.

**Rail:** The nearest main line railway station is Newcastle Central Station, around three miles away. Local trains call at Heworth Interchange.
The stadium has a Tyne & Wear Metro Station: the Gateshead Stadium Metro station. This is at Shelley Drive, a five minute walk from the ground.

**Bus:** Go North East operates the 93/3 'Loop' bus service, which provides access to the stadium from the Team Vallet, Gateshead Interchange, Heworth Interchange and the Queen Elizabeth Hospital in Sheriff Hall. Every 15 minutes during the day, and every 30 minutes in the evenings.

**Road:**
**From the North:** From Tyne Bridge, Gateshead (A167). Continue on the A167, entering Gateshead. At the edge of Gateshead town centre continue onto Gateshead Highway, A167 (signposted South Shields, Sunderland A184). At the junction for Gateshead town centre keep in right hand lane, then at the roundabout take the first exit onto Park Lane, A184 (signposted South Shields, Sunderland). Left onto Neilson Road leads to the stadium.

**From the South, A19:** Follow signs to the Tyne Tunnel. Bear left onto Newcastle road, A184, (signposted The South, Gateshead). Junction with A194(M) / A194 - continue straight across flyover. Continue onto the A184, entering Gateshead. Come to Heworth Metro station, at the roundabout take second exit continuing on the A184 (signposted Gateshead, Newcastle). Turn right onto Neilson Road which leads to the stadium.

**From the A1 (signposted The South, Gateshead):** Go on the Gateshead Western Bypass. Branch left, then merge onto the A184, (signposted Gateshead). At junction with A189 branch left , then at roundabout take third exit onto Askew Road, A184 (signposted Gateshead Town Centre). Bear left and then turn right onto Oakwellgate. Turn right onto Hawks Road. At traffic lights turn left onto Gateshead Highway, A167 signposted South Shields, Gateshead A184).Then as 'from North' above.

**Parking:** There is a free car park outside the main stand. This is usually more than adequate for regular league matches, but there are industrial estates surrounding the ground which offer an alternative.

## Halifax

**Ground:** The Shay Stadium
**Address:** Shay Syke, Halifax, West Yorkshire HX1 2YS
**Phone:** 01422 342 792
**Fax:** 01422 264 721
**Website:** www.halifaxrlfc.co.uk
**E-mail:** info@halifaxrlfc.co.uk
**Twitter:** @Halifax_RLFC
**Colours:** Home: Blue and White hoops, White shorts and Blue and white socks (hence the short-lived nickname the Blue Sox).
**Capacity:** 10,500. **Seats:** 5,830. **Standing:** 4,670.

**Stadium history:** Halifax RLFC is one of the most historic clubs in the game. Formed in 1873, Halifax were one of the 22 clubs that formed the Northern Union in 1895. They have been league champions four times and Challenge Cup winners five times.
The word 'Shay' is derived from the old English word 'shaw', which means a small wood, thicket or grove. Halifax RLFC shares the stadium with football club FC Halifax Town. The stadium is owned by Calderdale Metropolitan Council after the football club sold it in the 1980s to pay off debts. Halifax RLFC moved to the Shay in 1998 after selling their home at Thrum Hall. The club had been based there since 1886, but in 1998 it was sold to Asda for £1.5million. The proceeds from this sale were supposed to enable the club to complete a redevelopment of the Shay, but the money was swallowed by debts.

**The stadium:** The Shay has four stands: North stand – standing; South stand – Standing; East stand – seating; West stand (Skircoat) – seating. The Skircoat stand is the oldest remaining stand. The North and South stands were built in the mid-1990s; the East stand was opened in March 2010. Originally the stadium only had three stands, which limited the capacity to 6,500.However, by collaborating with the local council, the club were able to complete the East Stand, thereby increasing the capacity to 10,500. Away fans usually congregate in the North Stand, while standing home fans usually stand behind the posts in the opposite South Stand

**Ticket office:** The ticket office is open two hours before kick-off and is located by the main entrance in the East stand.

**Ticket prices:** The capacity of the Shay is 10,500, although for most home games only the East and South stands are open. There are no changes allowed between stands on a match day, though a South stand ticket can be upgraded to an East stand one at a cost of £3 at the ticket office. East stand: adult: £18; concession: £13; junior: £5. South stand: adult: £15;

concession: £10; junior: £5. Serving members of HM Armed Forces are allowed in free, go to the ticket office with a warrant card.

**Supporters with Disabilities:** There are 19 accessible parking spaces outside the East Stand to pre-order. There is accessible seating in the East and South Stands for home and away supporters: 19 on the Balcony and 17 at ground level. In the South Stand there are 10 at ground level.

**Club shop:** The club shop is located by the East stand reception, and opens on match-days two hours before kick-off and for half an hour after the game.

**Refreshments:** The East stand has one refreshment stand in each of its concourse areas, both selling a selection of food and drink. The South stand has one refreshment van which offers a range of food and drinks. The Shay has two supporters bars, one each in the East and South stands. Each bar is open on match days two hours before kick-off and for a short time after the game.

The Shay Hotel is the nearest pub to the ground, and is just outside the North Stand. Also recommended: The Westgate, Westgate; The Pump Room, New Road; The Shears Inn, 1 Paris Gates; The Three Pigeons, South Parade.

**Directions:**

**Rail:** Halifax station is walking distance from the ground. On leaving the station, go to the end of the car park. At the traffic lights turn left and go along Church Street for 600 yards. The stadium is on the right, opposite B & M Bargains.

**Bus:** Any bus to Halifax Bus Station. Once leaving the main exit (opposite Sainsbury's), turn right and walk along Church Street. The walk to the ground is around 15 minutes.

**Road:**
**From the West:** Leave the M62 at junction 24 and take the A629 into Halifax. Follow signs for Eureka and the Railway Station, and the Stadium is just before Eureka on the left.
**From the East:** Leave the M62 at junction 26 and take the A58 into Halifax, follow signs for Eureka and the Railway Station and the Stadium is 600 yards after Eureka on the right.

**Parking at ground:** Parking in the main East Stand car park is extremely limited and reserved for staff, sponsors and diners. Spaces will be available at a price of £3 on a first come, first served basis, but availability is rare at most home games.

**Parking nearby:** There is usually plenty of street parking available within five minutes' walk of the Shay. Check for permit or reserved areas.

## Hemel Stags

**Ground:** Pennine Way Sports Ground
**Address:** Pennine Way, Hemel Hempstead HP2 5UD
**Phone:** 01442 219799
**Fax:** 01442 249610
**Website:** www.hemelstags.com
**E-mail:** info@hemelstags.com
**Colours:** Blue and yellow
**Capacity:** 2,000. **Seats:** 400. **Standing:** 1,600.

**Club history:** Hemel Stags were founded in April 1981 as a pub team wearing borrowed shirts. The club has played in a number of leagues over the years, from the London League, MASWARLA (Midlands and South West Amateur Rugby League Association), National Conference League and the Alliance League. Most recently they have played in the Rugby League Conference. In 2013 they are playing in Championship One, as one of three new entrants to that league.

**Stadium history:** Hemel Stags have been based at the Pennine Way stadium since they were formed in 1981. In 2008 the club obtained planning permission for a small stadium at Pennine Way, and the first stage was completed in 2010 with the enclosure of the ground and the floodlighting of the main pitch. In preparation for Hemel's admittance to Championship 1 in 2013, a 400 seat stand was built at the end of the 2012 season. The stand is currently open, with plans to cover it.

**The stadium:** Bypassing the town's famous landmark, the Magic Roundabout, Pennine Way lies on the outskirts of town, close to the village of Redbourn. There is a sizeable clubhouse with roomy changing rooms, and the pitch is well maintained by the newly-erected stand.

**Ticket prices:** Adults: £12; concessions: £6; under-16: £1.

**Supporters with disabilities:** Very much, like the whole club, a work in progress. Presumably wheelchairs could use the area in front of the stand. No disabled toilet as yet.

**Refreshments:** There is a function room with a bar open seven days a week. Good bar facilities and pre-match lunch on offer as part of the hospitality package. There are bar snacks and on match days burgers, sausages and chips available from the kitchen in the clubhouse.

**Directions:**

**Rail and bus:** Hemel Hempstead station is on the Euston to Northampton line. A taxi to the ground is £7 to £8.
Buses are frequent from outside the station and most stop in the town centre, from where a 4 or 5 goes to Pennine Way. Ask for Redbourn Way

because it is better known to drivers. Get off the bus outside MFI. Fares are around £1.50 one way.
From Hemel Hempstead station Bus 2 departs from Stop F and goes to Fletcher Way, Bellgate Shops, from where it is a short walk to Pennine Way.

**Road:**
From the M1: Take junction 8, follow A414 into Hemel Hempstead. Go straight at the first roundabout. At the second roundabout turn right onto Maylands Avenue (A4147). At the next roundabout turn left, still on A4147. At fourth roundabout, turn right onto Redbourn Road. Pennine Way is 250 yards on the left after the Ford garage.
From the A41: Follow the signs to the M1. At the first roundabout ('Funny Roundabout') take the M1 exit. At the second roundabout (Tesco) go straight on. At the third roundabout go straight on. At fourth roundabout turn left into Maylands Avenue (A4147). At next roundabout turn left. At next roundabout turn right onto Redbourn Road. Pennine Way is 250 yards on the left after the Ford Garage.

**Parking:** There is some parking at the ground and on Pennine Way, although the facilities are limited and would struggle with a large crowd.

The stand at Pennine Way – the home of Hemel Stags.

# Huddersfield Giants

**Ground**: John Smith's Stadium
**Address:** Stadium Way, Huddersfield, HD1 6PG
**Phone:** 01484 484 100
**Fax:** 01484 481 184
**Website:** www.giantsrl.com
**E-mail:** enquiries@giantsrl.com
**Twitter:** @GIANTSRL
**Colours:** Home: Claret and Gold; Away: Blue and Gold
**Capacity:** 24,500 (all seated)

**Club history:** Huddersfield are one of the original clubs that formed the Northern Union in 1895. The club were founded in 1864, which makes them one of the world's oldest rugby league teams. With a trophy haul of seven Championships and six Challenge Cups it is also one of the most successful clubs in the game. The club, particularly among older supporters, is often referred to locally as Fartown, named after the ground which they occupied until 1992, which was located in the Fartown district of Huddersfield.

**Stadium history:** The stadium is shared with Huddersfield Town Football Club. Originally called the Alfred McAlpine Stadium, it was re-named the Galpharm Stadium in 2004 after a sponsorship deal with Galpharm Healthcare. It subsequently became the John Smith's Stadium. It was a joint venture with the Council, and includes a cinema, gym and education facilities on site.

**The stadium:** Each stand is semi-circular rather than rectangular, further enhanced by large white steel tubing above the contours. Indeed, the ground has won numerous design awards. However, one disappointment is that the corners of the ground are open. The Fantastic Media North Stand at one end and the Direct Golf UK (Riverside) stand at one side are both two-tiered stands.
The other two sides of the ground are large, single-tiered affairs. One of these, the Britannia Rescue stand, can hold 7,000 fans.
As an all-seater football stadium, it is no surprise to find clear views all round and the leg room is decent too. Home fans are allowed in the Direct Golf, Britannia Rescue Stand and Fantastic Media Lower Tier Stands. Away fans are located in the John Smith's Stand.

**Ticket office:** Supporters can purchase tickets by calling the ticket office on 01484 484 123 or online: www.eticketing.co.uk/huddersfieldgiants
The ticket office is open: Monday to Friday: 9am to 5pm. Saturday: 9am to midday. Sunday matchdays from 11am through to kick-off, and 30 minutes after the game.

**Ticket prices:** adults: £21 (pre purchase), £24 (match day); concessions: £15 (pre-purchase), £18 (match day); juniors (12 to 16) £5 (pre-purchase), £8 (match day); under-12s: free. Once in the ground no movement between stands is allowed.

**Supporters with disabilities:** For any enquiries about access for disabled supporters contact ticket office administrator Rachel Chambers , tel: 01484 484159, e-mail: rachel@giantsrl.com
There are 44 matchday disabled parking spaces available in the St Andrews Car Park, situated behind the John Smiths Stand: 18 on upper level of car park; 26 on lower level. These are allocated on a first come, first-served basis. For wheelchair-bound supporters there are designated seats in the Britannia Rescue Stand, the John Smith's Stand and the Direct Golf Lower Tier.
Match Commentary is available for visually impaired supporters and can be accessed through the stadium reception. The equipment is wire-free, and can be used in all areas of the stadium
Disabled supporters have access to toilets specifically designed for their use. There are 13 in total, including two in the John Smiths Stand.
Prices: ambulant disabled and visually impaired £21 (pre-purchase), £24 (match day) with helper free. Wheelchair disabled: £15 (pre-purchase), £18 (match day) with helper free. The first price is pre-purchase; the second matchday prices.

**Club shop:** The club shares a shop with Huddersfield Town, where which is open during the week as well as on match-days, open Monday to Friday 9am to 5pm and Saturdays 9am to midday.
Online: www.giantsrl.com/shop
The clubs also have a shop in the town centre called the Sporting Pride store, at 12 Cloth Hall Street, open Tuesday to Saturday 9am to 5pm.

**Refreshments:** Outlets in all stands which serve a range of food and drink. There are also match day hospitality facilities available, contact the club for details.

**Local refreshments:** The Bradley Mills Working Mens Club and Ricky's Bar are both located on Leeds Road, and are a five to 10 minute walk from the stadium. There is also a cinema and entertainment complex behind the North Stand, where there is the Rope Walk Pub.
Walking from the station, come along Leeds Road, which has quite a few pubs within a 10-minute walk from the ground. There is a wide range of takeaways, cafes and restaurants in the town centre.

**Directions:**

**Rail:** The stadium is in walking distance from Huddersfield Railway station, and should take about 15 minutes. After coming out of the station, turn

down past the front of The George Hotel. Go straight over the crossroads into Northumberland Street and walk down across the ring road on into Leeds Road. Turn right down Gasworks Street, and straight over the crossroads to the ground.
**Bus:** There are numerous buses from the Bus Station. Ask for one that runs along Leeds Road past the Stadium. The Bus Station is 400 metres from the train station. Ring West Yorkshire Metro on 0113 245 7676

**Road:** The stadium is just off the A62 Leeds Road. From M62, junction 25, follow the signs for Huddersfield via the A62, and the stadium is on the left.
**From the South:** Leave the M1 at junction 38 and take the A637 towards, and then the A642, into Huddersfield. When approaching the town centre try to keep in the right hand lane, turn right at the roundabout onto the A62 Leeds Road. The stadium is a short distance down this road on the right.

**Parking:** For the car parks turn right at the traffic lights on the A 62, where the Market Pub is on the corner.
The stadium is well signposted around Huddersfield Town Centre. There is good size car park at the ground, and there are a number of other car parks nearby, all of which charge on match days.
There is a large car park just outside the stadium complex which is good for getting away afterwards

**Sporting attractions: The George Hotel**
Opposite the railway station in St George's Square, The George Hotel is a Grade 2 listed building built in 1851. It was at the George Hotel, on 29 August 1895, that 21 northern rugby union clubs held a meeting, and by a majority of 20 to 1 voted to secede from the Rugby Football Union to set up their own Northern Rugby Football Union. In 1922 this became the Rugby Football League.
The Rugby League Heritage Centre was opened in 2005 in the basement of the George. Within the Centre were displays of memorabilia, films and a small rugby league bookshop. However, the hotel closed suddenly in January 2013 due to financial problems and its future, and the future and venue of the Heritage Centre are unclear at the time of writing.

# Hull FC

**Ground:** Kingston Communications Stadium, usually referred to as the KC Stadium.
**Address:** The Circle, Walton Street, Hull HU3 6HU
**Phone:** 01482 327200
**Website:** www.hullfc.com
**E-mail:** info@hullfc.com
**Twitter:**
**Colours:** White and Black
**Capacity:** 25,404 (all seated)

**Club history:** In 1865 a group of former schoolboys from York formed a rugby team. Soon another team, Hull White Star, was formed and the two clubs merged. Hull Football Club was one of the first clubs in the north of England to join the Rugby Football Union. They were one of the founding members of the Northern Union in 1895. Later that year they moved to the Hull Athletic Club's ground at The Boulevard, Airlie Street, which gave rise to their nickname 'The Airlie Birds'.
Traditionally, people from the west side of Hull support Hull FC, while Hull Kingston Rovers are supported by the east half, the 'border' is the River Hull.

**The stadium:** The KC Stadium was opened in December 2002, at a cost of £44m, and has the biggest capacity in Super League. The Stadium is totally enclosed, with the Cranswick plc (West) Stand being around twice the size of the other three sides. The roof rises up and curves around the Cranswick plc stand which gives the stadium an interesting look. Inside the curves continue as each of the stands slightly bows around the playing area, drawing the eye to sweep panoramically around them. Each stand is single-tiered, apart from the two-tiered West Stand. There is a large video screen at the North End of the stadium.
A bowl design, the North, East and South Stands are of similar height and design, with the two tiers of the main West Stand setting it apart.
The KC Stadium, well signposted once you enter Hull itself, is rather two-faced: approach from the east on a footbridge through an industrial estate and over a railway line and it's pretty grim. Come from the south-west and it's delightfully set in the corner of West Park, where Yorkshire played cricket until 1990. There is a memorial to Jack Harrison, a Hull player who was killed in the First World War and was awarded the Victoria Cross.
The stadium is shared with Hull City Football Club.

**Ticket office:** 01482 505 600. www.hullfc.com/page/996/match-day-tickets

**Ticket prices:** North Stand (away supporters) adult £23 pre-game, £24 game day; concession: £19; junior: £12. South Stand: adult: £19; concession: £15; student: 10; junior: £10; East Stand: adult: £24

(reserved), £23 unreserved); concession £19; junior £12; family £65 (two adults, two juniors).
West Stand: (reserved) adult: £24; concession: £19; junior: £14; family: one adult and one junior £25; two adults and two juniors £50.

**Supporters with disabilities:** Contact: Sue Smith on 01482 304951.
112 accessible car parking spaces in the Perimeter and South stand car parks for home supporters, and two for away supporters.
131 pairs of accessible spaces and seats for home wheelchair users and carers. (64 pairs undercover). Between 16 and 32 spaces and seats for away wheelchair users and carers, all undercover.
There are accessible toilets and refreshment counters located near the accessible seating. 20 head-sets available for audio commentary.

**Club shop:** KC Retail Store on match days. Savile Street store: Monday to Saturday: 9am to 5pm. Online: www.hullfcshop.com

**Refreshments:** There are food and drink facilities at the stadium, limited in the away supporters' area. Various matchday hospitality packages available.

**Local refreshments:** The ground is just a 10 to 15 minute walk from the city centre, so there are plenty of choices. The Admiral of the Humber is very popular, while the Eagle on Anlaby Road, is just five minutes from the ground. The Sports Bar outside the South End is members only, and fans can't take alcohol to their seats.

**Directions:**

**Air:** Humberside Airport is 18 miles from Hull. Phone: 01652 688456. www.humdersideairport.com Email: enquiries@humbersideairport.com

**Rail:** Hull Paragon Station is less than a mile away with well sign-posted footpaths leading to the Stadium. The Stadium is around a 20 minute walk away from the station. Turn left at the end of the railway station platforms, and then left into the bus station without going outside the station. Exit the bus station at the far end. Walk past Tesco on the right, cross over Park Street at the traffic lights. Following blue pedestrian signs to KC Stadium along Londisborough Street (where there is a handy fish and chip shop) Cross Argyle Street and onto pedestrian walkway and bridges over railway lines to the Stadium.

**Bus:** Hull bus/coach station is located next to Paragon Station, less than one mile from the stadium. Frequent bus services run along Spring Bank and Anlaby Road. Phone: 01482 222222

**Road**

**From the West:** Approach Hull from the M62, which leads straight onto the A63. Continue on the A63 under the Humber Bridge. The road continues into the A63 Clive Sullivan Way.

Continue along Clive Sullivan Way. Turn off onto the slip road just before the fly-over, sign-posted 'Local Traffic/Infirmary' and for KC Stadium. At the roundabout, take the second exit, Rawling Way. At the next set of traffic lights (and with the hospital straight ahead) take a left turn onto A1105 Anlaby Road. Continue over the flyover. At the foot of the flyover, take a left turn into Walliker Street. Once on Walliker Street, take the next immediate left turn onto Carnegie Street, and then another left onto Perry Street. Follow Perry Street around and under the flyover. Once under the flyover, take a right turn and the Stadium's car parks are in front of you.

**From the Humber Bridge:** Once over the Humber Bridge, follow signs for Hull City Centre. The road follows round to the left to join the A63 Clive Sullivan Way and will take you under the Humber Bridge. Continue along Clive Sullivan way...and then as above.

**From the North:** Take the A1079 towards Beverley then follow signs for the Humber Bridge and the A164. Take the A63 sign-posted Hull City Centre. Continue on the A63 under the Humber Bridge. The road continues into the A63 Clive Sullivan Way – and then as for 'From the West'.

**From the East and Hull Docks:** The A165 approaches Hull from the East Coast and onto Holderness Road. Follow signs for A63/M62 Leeds. At the second large roundabout on the A63 Garrison Road, continue over Myton Bridge straight onto A63 Castle Street. Continue along the A63. Just before the flyover, take the slip road signposted 'Infirmary/Anlaby A1105', and at the roundabout take the third exit onto Rawling Way. Then as 'From the West'.

**Parking at ground:** Between the ground and the train station is the Infirmary. It has a pay and display section, but can take a little while getting out of afterwards.
Priory Way park and ride is probably the best way when travelling from outside Hull. After going under the Humber Bridge on the A63, take the first exit and turn left. Take the first right and the car park is on the right. Buses from here to the town centre travel down Anlaby Road past the KC Stadium. Executive and guest parking only at the stadium and parking around the ground is severely limited. It is nearly all double yellow lines or residents-only.

**Parking nearby:** The Walton Street fairground site has 1,100 spectator parking spaces. There are numerous city centre car parks which are a 10 to 15 minute walk from the stadium using the sign-posted routes.

## Hull Kingston Rovers

**Ground:** MS3 Craven Park
**Address:** MS3 Craven Park Stadium, Preston Road, Hull, East Yorkshire HU9 5HE
**Phone:** 0844 2490 105
**Fax:** 01482 791.586
**Website:** www.hullkr.co.uk
**E-mail:** info@hullkr.co.uk
**Twitter:** @hullkr_online
**Colours:** Home: Red and white; away: blue.
**Capacity:** 10,000.

**The stadium:** Hull KR joined the Northern Union in 1897, and have become one of the sport's great clubs. Along with neighbours Hull FC, their best period was in the 1980s, when the two clubs dominated the sport, including meeting in the 1980 Challenge Cup Final which the club won 10–5. After a fallow period, they are now established in Super League.
Craven Park is Rovers' ninth home, and they have been here since 1989. When Craven Park was built Rovers had to share, first with greyhound racing and then speedway, which may account for the layout. Now with those two sports gone, the club is (at the time of writing) building a new North Stand behind the tryline. The view from up above in the lofty West Stand astride the halfway line reveals acres of flatlands and, to add a Dutch flavour near the Rotterdam ferry terminal, a wind turbine.

**Ticket office:** The North Stand, when completed, will house away fans and provide new corporate facilities. Away fans can use the south terrace or sit in parts of The Well. Tickets are only available from the ticket office on 01482-374162.

**Ticket prices: East Stand:** adult: £22; concession: £15; youth: £12; junior: £11; under five: free.
**Roger Millward West Stand:** adult: £25; concession: £19; youth: £13; junior: £12; under five: free. (Limited availability in block C)
**Roger Millward The Well:** adult: £22; concession: £15; youth: £13; junior: £12; under five free.

**Supporters with disabilities:** Contact: Dave Bradley on 01482 708901 Dave.bradley@hullkr.co.uk Parking is allocated on a first-come, first-served booking system, and home and away supporters are encouraged to book a space.
Home fans have a choice of area: The Harry Poole Disabled viewing area is inside, and offers a view of the pitch from the first floor. Some restricted viewing. The East Stand disabled viewing area is situated at the south-east corner. It has a roof and side shelter from the elements. It is at pitch-level

and pitch-side. The Well disabled viewing area is situated at the south-west corner and again offers a roof and side shelter from the wind at a pitch-side level. For away fans the disabled viewing area is next to the West Stand disabled viewing area, located in the south-west corner. All stands have accessible catering facilities. Accessible toilets are located within the Robins' Nest corridor, the north east corner well, the south west corner well, Harry Poole corridor and behind the East Stand pod.
Audio commentary available for home and away supporters. Assistance dogs welcome.

**Club shop:** Holderness Road Superstore, 269 Holderness Road, Hull, East Yorkshire HU8 8TD. Telephone: 0844 2490 105. E-mail: retail@hullkr.co.uk Opening Hours: Monday to Friday: 9.30am to 5.30pm. Saturday: 9am to 5pm. There is also a club shop at the ground and via the club website.

**Refreshments:** Located in the Roger Millward, West Stand, the Robins Nest is open to home and away fans three hours before kick-off. Snack bar in the South Stand. There are also match day hospitality packages available in the 10-5 suite in the West Stand. Details on the club website.

**Directions:**

**Rail and Bus:** Paragon Interchange is the city's public transport hub. For bus timetables call 01482 222222. www.hullcc.gov.uk The ground is nearly five miles from Hull station, use buses 10F, 40, 41 or 43 from Albion Street.

**Road:** M62 (eastbound) to Junction 38, leads into the A63. Continue on the A63, under the bridge and over the flyover, and continue over the roundabout, still on the A63. At the next roundabout exit the A63, and join the A1033 (Hedon Road). Follow the A1033 straight over the roundabout, and past Hull Prison. After about ¼ mile is another roundabout. Again head straight across, and 1,000 yards later, turn left at the roundabout into Marfleet Lane. At the next set of traffic lights, turn right onto the dual carriageway (Preston Road). MS3 Craven Park is about halfway down on the right hand side near the end of the dual carriageway.
Once past the city centre there are no signs for Craven Park. The first sign for the ground is on the roundabout off Hedon Road. The ground is deep in the housing estates of East Hull, on the edge of the city.

**Parking at ground:** £5 a car, in a large car park behind the main stand. There is only one access road onto Preston Road, and there are bad bottlenecks after matches.

**Parking nearby:** There is street parking around the ground but you may have to walk the best part of a mile on a busy match day.

# Hunslet Hawks

**Ground:** John Charles Centre for Sport (South Leeds Stadium)
**Address:** Middleton Grove, Leeds, West Yorkshire LS11 5DJ
**Phone:** 0113 271 2730
**Website:** www.hunslethawksrl.co.uk
**E-mail:** info@hunslethawks.co.uk
**Twitter:** @hunslethawksrl
**Colours:** Myrtle/Flame/White
**Capacity:** 3,450. **Seats:** 2,450. **Standing:** 1,000.

**Stadium history:** The John Charles Centre for Sport was previously named, and is often still known locally as the South Leeds Stadium. It was renamed to honour John Charles, the former Leeds United, Juventus and Wales footballer. There was disappointment among rugby league fans that the stadium was not named after a former Hunslet player.
In addition to the Hunslet Hawks, who have been there since November 1995, it is the principal athletics stadium in the Leeds area (and home of Leeds City Athletics Club) and has been used by Leeds United for reserve games. Moving to the stadium ended a nomadic period for the club after they lost their historic Parkside home in 1973.

**The stadium:** The ground has a modern, two-tiered stand with a capacity of 2,450. For the 2013 season 1,000 supporters will be able to stand on the grass bank opposite the stadium, raising the capacity above the 3,000 minimum required for Championship clubs.
Due to the running track surrounding the field there is a fair distance between players and spectators.

**Ticket prices:** adults: £12 to £16; concessions: £6 to £8 (65 and over); juniors: £3 (16 and under).

**Supporters with disabilities:** Contact: Peter Todd on 07827 325926. There are 28 reserved accessible parking spaces for home and 28 for away supporters. There are 10 accessible seats for home supporters and the same for away fans; all are under cover with an unobstructed view.
Refreshment, toilet and hospitality areas are all accessible.

**Club shop:** www.hunslethawks.co.uk There is also a matchday shop at the ground.

**Refreshments:** The Phoenix Bar: all fans welcome, no membership required. Walk through the Dug Out bar. Open from 12 noon on Sundays until kick-off, and then from the final whistle until late.
Snacks are also served from the kiosk on the top tier of the stadium.
There are matchday hospitality facilities available, including a carvery.

**Directions:**

**Rail:** Middleton station at Park Halt has limited access at weekends.

**Bus:** When opened the sports centre could only be accessed by car or by foot, at the end of a road serving a factory estate.
Since the road was extended through to Belle Isle, one bus route, 481 Leeds-Wakefield has been rerouted, providing a direct service from Leeds city centre, but only in the evenings and on Saturday. There are regular buses running on Dewsbury Road from destinations including Huddersfield Kirklees, and Moortown. It's then a five to 10 minute walk through the industrial estate.

**Road:**

**From the West:** Exit M62 at Junction 28. At roundabout first exit onto A653 signposted Leeds. At next roundabout take second exit onto A653 signposted Leeds. At next roundabout again take second exit onto A653 signposted Leeds. As road forks, branch right onto Dewsbury Road signposted Leeds South. After around one mile (having passed Tommy Wass pub on the left) turn right between the Kwik Fit garage and the Dewsbury Road Social Club onto Middleton Grove. The stadium is at the top of the hill on the left.

**From the East:** Leave the M62 at Junction 29 , then at roundabout take the third exit, then join the M1 motorway signposted The North.
Branch right onto the M621 signposted Leeds City Centre. Leave the M621 at Junction 5, then turn left into Tunstall Road, signposted Hunslet-Beeston.
At 2nd set of traffic lights turn left onto A653 Dewsbury Road.
After half a mile turn left at lights between Kwik Fit garage and Dewsbury Road Social Club onto Middleton Grove. The stadium is at the top of the hill on the left.

**From the South:** M1, then branch right onto the M621 signposted Leeds city Centre. Then follow instructions as above.

**Parking at ground:** Car parking at the stadium is free. However, the car park in front of the stadium has a three hour time limit.

## Keighley Cougars

**Ground:** Cougar Park
**Address:** Royd Ings Avenue, Keighley, West Yorkshire BD21 3RF
**Phone:** 01535 606044
**Fax:** 01535 609088
**Website:** www.keighleycougars.com
**E-mail:** enquiries@keighleycougars.com
**Twitter:** @Cougarmania
**Colours:** Home: Red, White, Green
**Capacity:** 7,800.

**The stadium:** Keighley RLFC was formed on 17 October 1876, and their first game took place a month later at Lawkholme Lane. The ground was sold in the late 1980s to the Co-op and leased back to the club. Having flirted with a winding-up order in the mid-1980s, the club was officially launched as The Cougars in August 1991. The renovation of the ground followed, and it became 'Cougar Park'.
The stadium has a main stand, cover behind one goal and open terracing.

**Ticket prices:** adult ground: £15; concession ground: £8; under-16 ground: free; stand transfer: £2. Tickets can be ordered online, although there is a small delivery charge. They can also be collected from the ground.

**Supporters with disabilities:** Contact: Gary Fawcett on 01535 606044. There are 200 accessible car parking spaces 300 yards away, with 30 per cent given to away supporters. There are 80 accessible seats for wheelchair users, split with half for away supporters. All seats have an unobstructed view, and each lot of 40 seats has 15 under cover. There are 100 accessible seats for the ambulant disabled, again split with half for away fans.
The Armour Glass Suite upstairs via the lift and Hall of Fame via the slope (ground level) are accessible. Assistance dogs are welcome.

**Club shop:** www.keighleycougars.com/shopping
There is also a club shop at the ground.

**Refreshments:** There are various bars at the ground, in the main stand, and other refreshment facilities. There are also hospitality facilities available; contact the club for details.

**Directions:**

**Rail:** Keighley, half a mile from the ground. Regular services from Leeds, Bradford and Skipton and infrequent services from Lancaster and Carlisle.

**Bus:** 662 (Bradford) and 760 (Leeds). Alight by Netto Supermarket, 400 yards from the ground.

**Road:** From M62: Exit at junction 26. Take the M606 towards Bradford, heading towards the city centre. Follow the signs which lead onto the A650 through Shipley and Bingley. On the outskirts of Keighley, turn left at the roundabout after the Magnet showroom, heading towards Riddlesden. Follow this road for about 1.5 miles, and then turn right (third exit) at the next roundabout. The ground is on the left (behind a petrol station)

**Parking at ground:** Cars £2.
There is also parking in the sports centre across the road from the ground, and some local street parking.

# Leeds Rhinos

**Ground:** Headingly Stadium
**Address:** Headingly Stadium, St Michaels Lane, Headingley, Leeds LS6 3BR
**Phone:** 0844 248 6651
**Fax:** 0844 248 6652
**Website:** www.therhinos.co.uk
**E-mail:** info@leedsrugby.com
**Twitter:** @leedsrhinos
**Colours** Home: blue & yellow; away: pink & blue.
**Capacity:** 21,000.

**Club history:** In 1864 H.I. Jenkinson placed an advert in the *Leeds Mercury* inviting players to meet up at Woodhouse Moor a few days a week from 7am to 8am. That advert attracted over 500 members. From this interest several clubs were formed including Leeds St Johns, which was formed in 1870, under the Rugby Football Union. In 1895 Leeds were one of the original 22 clubs that broke away from the Rugby Union to form what is now the Rugby Football League. They have always been one of the sport's leading clubs.
Leeds won their first Challenge Cup in 1910, and have gone on to win it 11 times. However, the club did not win their first championship until 1961, and since then have won eight in total, as well as three World Club Challenge titles. Leeds were one of the original 12 Super League clubs when rugby league became a summer sport in 1996. The 'Rhinos' nickname and logo were introduced in 1997.

**Stadium history:** The first game was played at the stadium on 20 September 1890, when Leeds beat Manningham. The ground soon became the premier venue in Yorkshire, and the Yorkshire Cup Final was often held at Headingley, attracting crowds of over 14,000. In 1923, it was recorded that "ground improvements had seen the building of a ginnell wall with consequent additional terracing for 4,000 spectators."
The stadium has staged international matches and Challenge Cup Finals in the past. However, its limited seating capacity has meant that it has not staged major international matches in recent years. It was the first rugby league ground to install undersoil heating, which it did in 1963.

**The stadium:** The site is shared with Yorkshire County Cricket club, with one stand serving both venues. The cricket ground is a world famous international venue in its own right, and is Yorkshire's major ground. Headingley Stadium now has a capacity of 22,250, including both seating and standing areas. Headingley is the largest stadium in Super League not to be shared with a football club, although they do share with the Leeds Carnegie rugby union team. The new Carnegie stand was opened in 2006, with a capacity of 4,550 including 1,844 seats. It also includes a café bar and conference and meeting facilities used with Leeds Metropolitan University. The club are currently considering further modernisation. There is also a hotel on the site.

**Ticket office:** Monday to Friday: 9am to 5pm.
Friday (home matches) 9am to 20 minutes after final whistle. Saturday: 9am to midday. Sunday and bank holidays: Closed, unless match-day: two hours prior to kick-off to 20 minutes after final whistle .
Phone: 0871 423 1315. E-mail: tickets@leedsrugby.com
Tickets can be booked on line via the club website.

**Ticket prices: Carnegie Stand centre seats:** adult: £30; senior citizen, students, under-21s: £22; junior 12 to16: £21; junior under-12: £21.
**North Stand & Carnegie Stand wing seats:** adult: £27; senior citizen, students, under-21s: £19; junior 12 to16: £18; junior under-12: £18.
**Paddock seats:** adult: £23; senior citizen, students, under-21s: £16; junior 12 to16: £15; junior under-12: £15.
**Standing:** adult: £20; senior citizen, students, under-21s: £13; junior 12 to16: £12; junior under-12: £12.
There is a £1.50 charge for booking online, identification is necessary for age related & student concessions.

**Supporters with disabilities:** Leeds Rhinos offer disabled supporters a concessionary priced ticket (upon valid proof of disability). If disabled fans require assistance they will offer an additional ticket for a helper free of charge. The ground has several designated areas for its supporters who require a wheelchair. There is availability in the South Stand, Carnegie Stand upper (access by lift) and lower. The ground has good facilities for its disabled supporters with six toilets; these are located in the Carnegie Café bar, Carnegie Upper tier, South Stand and the Main Pavilion. For visually impaired fans there are wireless headsets which receive the local hospital radio signal for most home fixtures. These are available upon request from the main pavilion. There is an allocation of disabled parking spaces and 20 wireless audio units available for each match. It is advisable to book seven days prior to the match. Contact Steph Kinghorn on 0113 2033 270 or e-mail steph.kinghorn@leedsrugby.com

**Club shop:** The club's shops provide a wide selection of Leeds Rhinos (and Leeds Carnegie) merchandise. The on-site club shop is located next to the Ticket office, near Gate B. The city centre store is located in the St John's Centre. Headingley Carnegie Stadium shop: 0871 423 1515 (option 3)
Website: www.store.leedsrugby.com
Hours same as ticket office City Centre shop: Phone: 0113 242 6156

**Refreshments:** There are public bars situated around the ground which serve a range of hot and cold drinks along with snacks. For corporate guests, the hospitality suites are situated in the Pavilion, or the Lewis Jones

Suite in the Carnegie stand or the Long Bar in the cricket East Stand. The public bars open at home games include the Sports Bar and Grandstand Bar in the Main Stand, the South Stand Bar, the Carnegie Café Bar, and the Long Bar is open after the game.

**Local refreshments**
Trio, 44 North Lane, Headingley, 0113 203 6090. Pizza, Pasta & Burgers
Flying Pizza, 60 Street Lane, Roundhay, 0113 266 6501. Italian
ARC, 19 Ash Road, Headingley, 0113 275 2223. Ideal for a pre-game drink
Box, 8 Otley Road, Headingley, 0113 224 9266. Vibrant bar with big screens.
Original Oak, 2 Otley Road, Headingley. 0113 275 1322. Traditional Pub

**Directions:**

**Air:** Leeds/Bradford Airport is a short cab ride away from the stadium.

**Rail:** Leeds City station is in the city centre, on the East Coast Main Line and Virgin Trains. The nearest stations to Headingley are Burley Park and Headingley, both about five minutes walk from the ground. Trains run regularly from Leeds City every 20 minutes, but check times after evening matches, when there is a more limited service.
www.eastcoast.co.uk www.virgintrains.co.uk

**Bus:** The following buses go near the ground: 1, 18, 18A, 28, 56, and 97. See the First Group web site: www.firstgroup.com/leeds

**Road:**
Leave the M62 at Junction 27. Pick up the M621, leaving it at Junction 2: signposted to Headingley Carnegie Stadium. Follow the A643 (A58) Wetherby Road. At the next roundabout take the City Centre/Wetherby A58 exit. Almost immediately, bear left to Ilkley (A65) and the airport. At the lights (TGI Friday on the left) turn left into Kirkstall Road A65. Go straight for about 800 yards. There is a sign at the traffic lights: Headingley 1.5 miles. Stay in the right hand lane. Turn right and go up the hill to another set of lights at the crossroads. Carry straight up Cardigan Road (Co-op on the left). After the pedestrian lights and bus stop turn left into St Michael's Lane, signposted Headingley Stadium. The ground is on the right.

**Parking at ground:** Car parking at Headingley Carnegie Stadium is very limited. There is parking at Easy Space car park on Burley Road, but only available on a season basis. Otherwise arrive early and hope for a place in the streets around Headingley.

**Taxis:** Taxis have a pick up and drop off point outside the stadium near Gate B.

**Sporting attractions:** Royal Armouries Museum, Armouries Drive, Leeds LS10 1LT. 0113 220 1999. Britain's national museum of arms and armour, over 8,500 objects. Open daily from 10am to 5pm, admission free.

## Leigh Centurions

**Ground:** Leigh Sports Village
**Address:** Sale Way, Leigh, Greater Manchester, WN7 4JY
**Phone:** 01942 487887
**Fax:** 01942 487889
**Website:** www.leighcenturions.com
**E-mail:** enquiries@leighrl.co.uk
**Twitter:** @LeighCenturions
**Colours:** Red and white
**Capacity:** 12,500; **seats:** 10,000; **standing:** 2,500.

**Stadium history:** The club was founded in 1878 as Leigh RFC and is one of the original 22 clubs that formed the Northern Union in 1895. Leigh won the Rugby League Championship in 1982 and the Challenge Cup in 1971. The club adopted the name Centurions for the 1995–96 season.
Leigh moved into their current stadium in December 2008. The old ground at Hilton Park has been demolished and the land sold for housing. The stadium forms part of the Leigh Sports Village Complex, which was opened by the Queen in May 2009. It is hoped that the new stadium will be the cornerstone of Leigh's application for a Super League franchise. England international matches have been played at the stadium, and for 2013 it is being shared by Swinton Lions.

**The stadium:** Leigh Sports Village is a development south west of Leigh town centre, on the north side of the Leeds and Liverpool Canal, close to Pennington Flash Country Park and accessed from the A579, Atherleigh Way and by pedestrian routes from the town and surrounding area. The main focus of the sports village is the stadium.
It is all seating in the West, East and South stands, with standing in the North stand. The Leigh East amateur rugby league club is also part of the sports village complex. There is also a sixth form college and a Morrison's supermarket on the site.

**Ticket office:** Opening hours: Mon-Fri 9am to 5pm (except Monday 4pm), Saturday 9am to midday.

**Ticket prices:** There is a saving of £2 off the cost of an adult ticket and £1 off the cost of a concession ticket with pre-purchased tickets. North and West stands: adult: £14; concession: £7; under-16: £5; under-12: £1.

**Supporters with disabilities:** There are a total of 109 disabled or easy access parking spaces in the stadium car parks, 24 of which are directly in front of the West Stand. Within the stadium there are a total of 74 disabled seats, accompanied by 74 seats for family or carers. Some of these seats are elevated with the remainder located at pitch level. All locations provide a clear and unobstructed view of the playing area and can be accessed via four lifts or the front loading entrances.

**Club shop:** Phone: 01942 487 892. www.leighrl.rstore.co.uk

**Refreshments:** There is the Legends Bar, on the north corner of the Main Stand, which has live sport on the television. There are also hospitality packages available, including pre-match meals. The kiosks in the ground offer a variety of refreshments and drinks, and look out for the 'meal deals' and the pies (the stadium is in the borough of Wigan!).

**Local refreshments:** The Railway, a little way up Atherleigh Way, is popular, or there is a Harvester on the retail park opposite. The Marstons Whiting Wren House has recently opened in Leigh Sports Village.

**Directions:**

**Rail:** Atherton station is approximately four miles from Leigh Sports Village, with services running regularly from the Greater Manchester area. Bus stops are close to the train station, with the 582 service to Leigh town centre running every 10 minutes.

**Bus:** Leigh Sports Village has its own bus stop outside the stadium which is served by route 597. Other routes and services include 34, 598 and 600 from Leigh Bus Station, which run every 30 minutes, and are within walking distance of the stadium.

**Road:**
Leigh Sports Village is just five minutes from Leigh Town Centre. Situated on Atherleigh Way (A579) just off A580 East Lancs Road, it is easily accessible from the M6, M60, M61 and M62. For Sat Nav, the postcode is WN7 4GY.

**Parking:** Leigh Sports Village has over 900 parking spaces, of which 99 are disabled spaces. On matchdays, approximately 800 spaces are available for spectators.

**Parking nearby:** Alternative car parking is also available in Leigh town centre.

## Leigh Sports Village

The entrance to the main stadium – the home of Leigh Centurions.

Amateurs Leigh East also play at the complex, and here are playing The Army in the Challenge Cup in March 2013.

## London Broncos

**Ground:** Twickenham Stoop Stadium
**Stadium address:** Langhorn Drive, Twickenham, Middlesex TW2 7SX
**Office address:** London Broncos, Richard Evans Playing Fields, Roehampton Vale, London SW15 3PQ
**Phone:** 020 8394 6160,
**Hospitality:** 020 8394 6161
All ticketing enquiries, including season tickets, are dealt with at the Twickenham Stoop Stadium on 020 8410 6000.
**Website:** www.londonbroncosrl.com
**E-mail:** info@londonbroncosrl.com
**Twitter:** @LondonBroncosRL
**Colours:** Black, sky blue, silver.
**Capacity:** 14,410 (all seated)

**Club history:** The club was formed as Fulham and entered the RFL Second Division for the 1980–81 season. Over the years the club has changed name a number of times and has been known as London Crusaders, London Broncos (up until 2006 and from 2012) and Harlequins Rugby League. London's rugby league club has never won a major trophy, but were Second Division champions in 1982–83, Divisional Premiership runners-up in 1994, Super League runners-up in 1997 and did reach the final of the Challenge Cup in 1999.

**Stadium history:** In 1963 Harlequins RUFC acquired an athletics ground with 14 acres, just over the road from the Twickenham stadium. This ground was used as their training pitch. This subsequently became Harlequin's permanent home, known for many years as the Stoop Memorial Ground, before being named the Twickenham Stoop in 2005, after Adrian Dura Stoop, who played 182 times for Quins between 1901 and 1939. London Broncos have announced that 2013 may be their last season at The Stoop.

**Stadium description:** To accommodate the expanding union fan base, the Twickenham Stoop has undergone a huge development in the past decade, doubling its capacity to 14,410. Before the redevelopment, there was one stand, and a temporary stand on the other side of the pitch. Teams even had to share toilets. Legend has it, if you were making any noise, people would tell you to keep quiet.

**Ticket prices:** adult (16 to 59): £20; senior citizens (60+) and students: £12; junior: (under-19): £5. £3 fee for booking online, students must provide ID.
For most rugby league matches, only the LV and Etihad Stands along the side of the pitch are open. Season ticket holders now have reserved seats in the LV (West) Stand. Away supporters usually go in the Etihad Stand.

Tickets can be purchased by calling the Ticket Office on 0871 527 1315, by booking online, or at the Ticket Office: Monday to Friday: 9am to 4pm. Matchdays: from two hours before kick-off from ticket office in south-east corner of stadium.

**Supporters with disabilities:** Seating for wheelchair users and disabled supporters is located in the front row of the Etihad stand. There are disabled toilets and the food kiosks and bars are also accessible.

**Club shop:** The club shop is open on match days. Otherwise, there is an on-line service for rugby league items.

**Refreshments:** The Kings Bar and Members Bar serve draught beers, bottled beers, wine, spirits and soft drinks. At corners of ground there are hot food vendors, including burgers, fish and chips and hog roast. The bar in the LV stand also serves pies, pasties and tea and coffee.

**Local refreshments:**
*The Scrummery* 105 Whitton Road, 020 8892 9797.
A bustling rugby café perfect for a pre-match breakfast or lunch.
*The Albany* 1 Queens Road, 0208 891 1777. Twickenham's first gastro-pub.
*Ozon* 33-35 London Road, 0208 891 3611, Good value Asian food.
*The Cabbage Patch,* 67 London Road, 020 8892 3874.
Considered *the* rugby pub in Twickenham.
*The William Webb* 24 London Road, 0208 744 4300.
Based in a former bank, there is plenty of room and live TV sport.
*The Garryowen* 68 London Road, 020 8892 3328.
Close to Twickenham station, and open until 2am on Saturdays.
There is also a nice café by Twickenham station which is a good place to meet before going to the ground.

**Directions:**

**Rail:** Twickenham station is served by trains from London Waterloo and Reading, with more services and routes accessible via Clapham Junction.
If on the underground, travel to Richmond and then there are regular local and fast trains to Twickenham. Six trains an hour.
(N.B. Even for occasional travellers in London, a pay-as-you-go Oyster card is considerably cheaper than paper tickets, and can be used in the Grater London area on trains as well as the underground and buses.)
On leaving the station, turn right towards Twickenham Rugby Stadium, cross the road and left at the traffic lights. Take the first left into Court Way and then turn left into Craneford way and continue on until you reach the stadium. The Twickenham Stoop is at the end of the road on the right.
About 10 minutes walk.

**Bus:** Bus number 267 runs between Hammersmith and Fulwell Garage. Bus number 281 runs between Hounslow and Tolworth. Both services stop near of the ground, the 267 at Twickenham station and the 281 in Whitton Road

**Road:**

**From the M3:** Follow the M3 until it ends at the Sunbury Roundabout. Continue up the A316 Chertsey Road, over three roundabouts. Continue for two miles. With Twickenham Stadium on the left, the Stoop is on the right. U-turn at the RFU roundabout. Enter the Stoop via Langhorn Drive, 450 yards on your left.

**From the M4:** Leave the M4 at Junction 3. Take the third exit off the roundabout for the A312, towards Feltham (A3006). Continue along the A312 for 4.5 miles. At the A305/A316 roundabout, turn left onto the A316. Then as from the M3.

**From the M1:** Either take the North Circular (A406) and then the South Circular (A205) and fork right onto the A307 towards Richmond, then go south on the A316. However, the traffic can be quite bad, and it can be as quick, albeit a bit further, to use the M25 to come into London on the M4, then as above.

**Parking:** There is ample parking at the Stoop. It costs £5 to park in the Rosebine next to the ground on the A316 and the same in the Richmond College car park. There are considerable restrictions on street parking, although there are a few spaces that are free on Sundays by Richmond College. Check for events at Twickenham Stadium, which can add enormously to the traffic.

**Sporting attractions:** Museum of Rugby, Twickenham Stadium 0208 892 8877. The Stoop does not have its own museum, but on the other side of the A316, accessible by footbridge, is the Museum of Rugby (Union) at Twickenham. Entry is £7 for adults, £5 for concessions. The Museum is very good, allow at least two hours. Saturday 10am to 5pm, Sunday 11am to 5pm. It is possible to upgrade to a stadium tour, but it's advisable to book that in advance. Tours and museum: £15, concessions £9, family ticket £45. (2013 prices)
Check the museum website via www.rfu.com for more details.

(N.B. if on the stadium tour, look out for the picture of Halifax versus York; both clubs switched to the Northern Union in 1895...)

## Rugby league in London

The main stand at The Stoop, the current home of the London Broncos.

The entrance to the London Skolars' New River Stadium.

## London Skolars

**Ground:** The New River Stadium (also known as White Hart Lane Community Sports Centre)

**Address:** White Hart Lane Community Sports Centre, White Hart Lane, Wood Green, London N22 5QW
**Phone:** 020 8888 8488
**Website:** www.skolarsrl.com
**E-mail:** info@skolarsrl.com
**Twitter:** @LondonSkolarsRL
**Colours:** Black, with red horizontal stripes
**Capacity:** 5,000; **Seats:** 1,040; **Standing:** 3,960.
The standing terrace is only made available when the main stand is full.

**Club history:** London Skolars were founded in 1995 for post-university players in London. The club quickly went "open", and have been semi-professional since 2003. The club name was changed into London Skolers in 1997 as they nearly got a big sponsorship from Skol.

**The stadium:** White Hart Lane Community Sports Centre (formerly New River Stadium) is set in 40 acres of landscaped parkland. It is one of Haringey's most grassed areas. The complex itself houses an athletics track, football and rugby pitches, tennis courts and a state of the art 3g multi-use games area.

**Ticket office:** The ticket office is open at least two hours before kick-off and is located just inside the main entrance to the stand.
Tickets can be purchased in advance from the club office, or online.

**Ticket prices:** adult: £12; concessions (senior citizens, students, under-16s): £6.

**Supporters with disabilities:** There are 12 accessible car parking spaces split 50/50 with away fans, 100 metres from the stadium. There are 10 accessible bays for wheelchair users split with half for away fans in the main stand, all under cover. The refreshment areas are accessible.

**Club shop:** Merchandise stall is situated in the Olympic Suite. Also online via the club website.

**Refreshments:** The Olympic Suite is situated under the main stand, where the catering kiosk is located. Next to the kiosk is the Olympic Bar, which is generally open from a couple of hours before kick-off until an hour or so after the final whistle.

**Directions:**

**Rail:**

**Underground:** The Skolars Stadium is located approximately one mile from Wood Green station on the Piccadilly line. Walk north on High Road (A105) and turn right into White Hart Lane.

**Train:** Bowes Park station is 20 minutes walk from the stadium. Go east on Myddleton Road, turn right on High Road and left into White Hart Lane.

**Bus:** W3 bus from Wood Green station drops off very close to the stadium and, for the Friday Night Lights match, Skolars run a courtesy bus to and from the stadium.

**Road:** M1 south to Junction 2, take exit onto A1 to the junction with the North Circular (A406). Keep on North Circular. Turn right on A105 at traffic lights. Turn left into White Hart Lane. The Stadium is on the left hand side 0.5 miles down White Hart Lane.
Or: From M25 junction 25 go south on A10; cross North Circular at roundabout, and continue south on A10. Turn right at traffic lights into White Hart Lane, pass Haringey Borough FC ground on left, and stadium is on right hand side.
From South: Go north on A10 or A105, then as above.

**Parking:** There is pay and display parking in the car parks next to the main stand and some street parking.

## North Wales Crusaders

**Ground:** The Glyndwr University Racecourse Stadium
**Address:** Mold Road, Wrexham LL11 2AH
**Phone:** 0844 272 3232
**Website:** www.crusadersrl.com
**E-mail:** info@crusadersrl.com
**Twitter:** @NWCrusadersRL
**Colours:** Red and green
**Capacity:** 10,500 (all seated)

**Club history:** The ground was home to former Super League club Crusaders from 2010. But in 2011 Crusaders withdrew their Super League license application, and ultimately folded. 2012 saw the birth of a new club, North Wales Crusaders. They are a separate entity from the former club.

**Stadium history:** The stadium is also the home of Wrexham FC, and has in the past also staged rugby union, cricket, horse racing and music concerts. The stadium is the world's oldest international football stadium, having hosted Wales' first ever home international in 1877. It is the largest stadium in North Wales, and the fifth largest in Wales. The Glyndwr Racecourse Stadium was for years known as the Racecourse Ground. International rugby league has also been played at the ground.

**The stadium:** Mold Road Stand: An all-seater stand with disabled facilities. It is the newest stand with a capacity of 3,500. Eric Roberts (Builders) Stand: Situated behind the goal, this stand seats 3,800 spectators.
Yale Stand: The main stand is an all-seater, fully covered facility.
The two tiers provide a capacity of 4,200.
The Kop: Behind the goal it has a capacity of 5,000. However, its future status is uncertain and was shut down prior to being demolished.

**Ticket office:** Located in the club shop on Mold Road.

**Ticket prices:** Matchday prices: adult: £14 (advance booking £12); concessions £8 (advance booking £7); under-16s: £5; under-7s: free. Hospitality packages available, contact 08432 896407.

**Supporters with disabilities:** There are 45 disabled parking places available at the front of the Mold Road Stand. 20 are for away supporters. There are 45 accessible seats with 20 given to away fans. These are in the front row with an unobstructed view.
Refreshments are available in the stands which can be accessed from the disabled area. Accessible toilets are on the ground floor of the Mold Road Stand.

**Club shop:** Situated on the corner of Mold Road and Crispin Lane. Some items also available online via the club website.

**Refreshments:** There is a bar located in the Mold Road stand, although alcohol is not allowed within sight of the playing surface. Food and drink are available from the concession booths around the ground.
The Racecourse Ground claims to be the only football stadium in the country to have a pub on site, The Turf Hotel. On the way into town there is a Wetherspoons, the Elihu Vale. Further down the same street is the Horse and Jockey.

**Directions:**

**Rail:** Wrexham General station is located directly next to the ground. Direct trains run from Chester in the north and Birmingham to the south.

**Bus:** Take the bus to the centre of Wrexham. Head towards the prominent multi-storey car park, turn right along Mold Road and the ground is located half a mile along on the right hand side. The ground is so close to the town centre that there is no need to catch a bus.

**Road:** Take the A483 from Chester or Oswestry for Wrexham. Exit at the "Mold" junction onto the A541, Mold Road, and then follow the signs for 'Town Centre'. The Racecourse ground is on the left.

**Parking nearby:** There is more than enough parking space in Wrexham town centre. The prominent multi-storey car park is the best bet.

## Oldham Roughyeds

**Ground:** Whitebank Stadium
**Address:** Whitebank Road, Limehurst Village, Oldham OL8 3JH
**Office:** Lansdowne Road, Chadderton, Oldham, OL9 9EF
**Phone:** 0161 628 3677
**Fax:** 0161 628 5700
**Website:** www.roughyeds.co.uk
**E-mail:** oldhamrlfc@btconnect.com
**Twitter:** @Roughyeds
**Colours:** Red and white hooped jerseys, blue shorts, red socks
**Capacity:** 1,000.

**Stadium history:** Oldham is one of the original clubs that formed the Northern Union in 1895. 'Roughyed' is a nickname for a person from Oldham, derived from the rough felt used in the hatting industry which once employed many people in the area. Oldham left their traditional home of Watersheddings in 1997. The club then used eight grounds in 12 years, only one of which was in Oldham. The Roughyeds' first game at Whitebank was on 9 May 2010. The ground was previously used by Oldham Boro FC.

**The stadium:** Over 350 seats were acquired from Wilderspool Stadium in Warrington, and were installed by volunteers. Timber used in the building of the new Wembley Stadium was re-used in the Whitebank redevelopment.

**Ticket prices:** adults: £12; concessions £10; under-16s: £4.

**Club shop:** Items on sale on match days at ground, and via club website.

**Supporters with disabilities:** Contact: John McAndrew on 0161 628 3677. Parking next to turnstiles, 30 feet from accessible seating area, on a first-come, first-served basis; space for about 30 vehicles. There are six accessible seats in the West Stand, on a first-come, first-served basis. There are two accessible toilets, one at the end of the accessible seating area, one in social club. Catering facilities accessible. Assistance dogs are welcome.

**Refreshments:** Pie and peas on sale at the ground. Bar and hospitality packages including meals available.

**Directions:**

**Road:** Leave M60 at junction 22. Turn right onto A627 (Victoria Road). Continue on A627, go through 2 roundabouts, then turn right onto Wellington Road. Turn left into A627 (Oldham Road). Turn left onto Coal Pit Lane, take second right onto White Bank Road. Ground is on the right.

**Other transport:** Bus services, visit www.gmpte.com
Hollinwood tram stop is 1.3 miles from the ground.

# Oxford

**Ground:** Oxford University Rugby Football Club.
**Address:** Jackdaw Lane, Iffley Road, Oxford OX4 1EQ
**Phone:** 07933 481079 (Operations manager)
**Website:** www.oxfordrl.com
**E-mail:** info@oxfordrl.com
**Twitter:** @Oxford_RL
**Colours:** Home: Blue shirts, white shorts and Socks; away: Vivid Green
**Capacity:** At least 2,000.

**Club history:** Oxford University has played rugby league side since 1976, and in the RL Varsity match against Cambridge from 1981. Amateur rugby league is well established in the city. This new, semi-pro club joined Championship 1 in March 2013.

**Stadium history:** Oxford play at Iffley Road, best known for the athletics track where Sir Roger Bannister broke the four minute mile on 6 May 1954, which adjoins the Oxford University Rugby Union club ground where the team play. This is a famous rugby union venue where many famous players have played for and against the University club. It has been used for sport since November 1876. Lots of historic rugby union photos in the pavilion.

**The stadium:** The main stand has covered seating; a small covered stand runs the full length of the pitch on the other side, there are seats in front of the pavilion and plenty of uncovered standing room. Entrances on Iffley Road and off Jackdaw Lane.

**Ticket prices:** adults: £12; concessions (students, armed forces, police, senior citizens) £6; juniors £5; under-7 £1.

**Supporters with disabilities:** Small wheelchair area in front of main stand. Contact club for further information.

**Club shop:** By main stand.

**Refreshments:** Bar in the pavilion, with drinks and snacks. Burgers, tea and coffee and some drinks by side of main stand.

**Directions:**

**Rail:** Oxford Station is on the main line from Paddington. Exit the railway station and turn right toward the main road. Catch either the 4A,4B or 4C bus from the Frideswide Square stop to travel in the direction of Rose Hill. Disembark at the James Street stop on Iffley Road.

**Road:** From the north, use the M1 to junction 15a, exit onto A43 and take the M40 south. Exit at junction 9 and take A41/A34 Oxford and head towards Cowley and Henley. At roundabout take first exit onto Southern Bypass (A423). At next roundabout, take first exit onto Abingdon Road

(A4144). Turn right onto Weirs Lane (B4495) and continue on B4495. Turn left onto Iffley Road (A4158) and then left onto Jackdaw Lane.
From London and south: Enter Oxford by A40; at roundabout take A420 into city centre, at first roundabout turn left into Iffley Road (A4158).

**Parking at ground:** Limited parking at ground (£10), entrance off Jackdaw Lane, behind main stand. The car park opposite the entrance is for the local sports centre.
Try the council car park near Riverside Centre, on Donnington Bridge Road, south off Iffley Road, a five to 10 minute walk along Meadow Lane. NB Meadow Lane is blocked off for cars.

**Parking nearby:** Park and ride service in the city. Use Redbridge Park and Ride. Take bus into city centre and then catch the 3/N3 between the city centre and Iffley Road. From London, use Thornhill Park and Ride. Take bus to St Clements and walk to ground. There is very limited street parking near the ground, and much of the area is resident parking only.

Above: The main stand at Oxford University RFC, home to the rugby league team. Below: the pavilion.

# Rochdale Hornets

**Ground:** Spotland Stadium
**Address:** Sandy Lane, Rochdale OL11 5DS
**Phone:** 01706 648004
**Fax:**
**Website:** www.hornetsrugbyleague.co.uk
**E-mail:** info@hornetsrugbyleague.co.uk
**Twitter:** @RochdaleHornets
**Colours:** Blue
**Capacity:** 9,900. **Seats:** 8,002. **Standing:** 1,898

**The stadium:** The ground is shared with Rochdale FC. The completion of the 3,650 seater Willbutts Lane Stand during the 2000–01 football season meant that all four sides of the Spotland ground had been fully developed during the past decade. The Sandy Lane Stand is the only standing area.

**Ticket prices:** adult: £12; concession £8; under-16 £5. Family season tickets available.

**Supporters with disabilities:** There are 12 shared, accessible car parking spaces. There are 17 spaces for home supporters in the Main Stand and Pearl Street Stand, and 16 spaces for away fans at the Willbuts Lane end. Catering facilities are accessible. Accessible toilets on the first floor. Assistance dogs welcome.
72 places available for wheelchair-bound fans and helpers. Wheelchair Users are charged the concession price with the carer free of charge. Ambulant disabled are charged the appropriate rate for their ticket, but if they need a full-time carer to accompany them, the carer is admitted free of charge. Full details can be obtained from the main reception on 0844 826 1907

**Club shop:** via the club website and at the ground on match days.

**Refreshments:** The ground has two bars, the Ratcliffe Arms, which is built into the main stand at the main car park entrance to the ground.
The Studds Bar is under the Pearl Street Stand.

**Local refreshments:** The Rochdale delicacy seems to be pie and peas, inside or outside the ground. There is an excellent chippy on Willbuts Lane This is across the road from the entrances to the Westrose Leisure Stand. The Cemetery Pub is a fair size but a short walk from the ground. It can be found at the traffic lights on the approach to the ground. There is also the Church Pub on Willbutts Lane.

### Directions

**Rail:** The ground is around three miles from the station; taxis available. To walk, go straight across the roundabout into Maclure Road. After 300 yards, with Halfords on the right, turn left into Drake Street. After half a mile, turn right at the traffic lights onto the A58 dual carriageway and head towards the town centre. After half a mile, at a major traffic junction with two 'spire' sculptures, cross the road towards Asda into Dane Street. Follow round past Asda until a set of traffic lights, Bury Road on the left. Follow the road, Mellor Street, for half a mile until a mini-roundabout. Just after the mini-roundabout the road forks. Take the left onto Edenfield Road. After 100 yards turn left into Willbutts Lane, the ground is 150 yards on the left.

**Road:** Exit the M62 at Junction 20, and follow signs for Rochdale along the A627 (M). At the end of the A627 (M), turn left onto Edinburgh Way (A664). At roundabout go straight onto Roch Valley Way (B6452). At traffic lights cross Bury Road (B6222). The road becomes Sandy Lane and the stadium is on the right after around half a mile.

**Parking at ground:** Parking at the stadium is available for £3 a car.

**Parking nearby:** Parking nearby has been made a bit more complicated recently thanks to double yellow lines in Willbutts Lane and residents parking schemes. There is still a fair bit of street parking available on Sandy Lane, on the approach to the ground. For more street parking turn left at the Cemetery Pub. There is also a church on Willbutts Lane which charges for parking.

## St Helens

**Ground:** Langtree Park
**Address:** McManus Drive, St Helens WA9 3AL
**Phone:** 01744 455 050
**Website:** www.saintsrlc.com
**E-mail:** info@saintsrlc.com
**Twitter:** @Saints1890
**Colours:** Home: White jersey with red 'V', white shorts, white socks with red trim. Away: Blue jersey with white 'V' blue shorts
**Capacity:** 18,000; **seats:** 10,150; **standing:** 7,850.

**Club history:** St Helens were a founder member of the Northern Union. They have been league champions on 12 occasions and runners-up 12 times. St Helens are also the second most successful side in the Challenge Cup, their 12 wins placing them behind only their rivals Wigan, and have appeared in 21 finals.

**Stadium history:** St Helens moved to their current home, Langtree Stadium in January 2012. While the new stadium was being built they played the 2011 season at the Halton Stadium in Widnes. Until 2010, St Helens played at the Knowsley Road, which had been their home since 1890. In 2008 St Helens were warned by the RFL that the quality of their stadium was too poor for them to be given a licence to continue in the league. Thankfully for the Saints, they got planning permission for construction of a new ground. St Helens played their first league game at the ground in 2012, when they beat Salford City Reds. The highest attendance to date was 17,980 against Wigan Warriors on 6 April 2012.

**The stadium:** St Helens have followed fashion by building their new home on a brown field site in the town centre, and for a brand new stadium Langtree Park has as much heritage as could be reasonably expected. A statue of 'King' Keiron Cunningham stands on the roof of a turnstile entrance; the main entrance welcomes all to the Club of Legends since 1873; each bar named after one of them. On every few yards of concourse wall there hangs a massive pictorial tribute complete with biography and statistics. Inside the club shop is a micro-museum of memorabilia, including the tops of the old Knowsley Road posts. The stadium has two terraced stands and two seated, with a capacity of 18,000. The East stand and the two most easterly blocks of the North stand are allocated to away supporters.
The North and South stands are all seated, and the West stand is all standing. North Stand: 4,718 seats and 46 disabled seats. South Stand: 5,233 seats and 55 disabled seats. It also holds the club shop, a bar and club ticket office. East Stand: 81 seats, 3,899 standing, and 5 disabled seats. West Stand: 118 seats, 3,796 standing, and 29 disabled seats.

## St Helens' new home: Langtree Park

The Keiron Cunningham statue.

The main entrance to Langtree Park.

**Ticket prices:** For all areas family tickets are available in various combinations of adults and children, see the website for details, we recommend booking in advance.
Hattons Solicitors West Stand, East Stand and South family**:** adult: £21; concession & young adult (16 to 21): £15; junior: £10; family: £24.30 to £54. North Stand and Solarking South Stand allocated (prices vary for Bronze, Silver and Gold matches): adult: £22.50 (B), £25 (S), £27.50 (G); concession and young adult: £17, £19, £21; junior £10 (B), £12 (S & G); family: £29.25 to £67.50 (B), £33.30 to £77.40 (S), £35.55 to £81.90 (G). North Stand and Solarking South Stand unallocated: adult: £22.50; concession and young adult: £17; junior: £10; family: £29.25 to £67.50.

**Supporters with disabilities:** Wheelchair accommodation is provided at ground level around the playing area in front of all four stands. Wheelchair accommodation is also available on elevated platforms in the North, West and South stands. Accessible toilets are provided solely for use by disabled people throughout the stadium. There are dedicated accessible car parking spaces at the rear of the North-West and South-East stands, both accessed from Peasley Cross Lane. Currently no specific provisions in place for fans with hearing impairments. Fans with visual impairments accommodated in any stands. Audio commentary is available via the audio wire free device. Spectators who wish to use any of these facilities should contact the club ticket office on 01744 455052 or Geoff Ward on 07921 1158713, who co-ordinates these issues on the day.

**Club shop:** Saints Superstore at the ground, open Monday to Saturday, 9am to 5pm, later on evening match days. Buy online: www.saintssuperstore.com

**Refreshments:** Langtree Park is open to the public during the week. Visit the South Stand Side and Founders Café Bar. There are also match day hospitality packages available, and various bars and food facilities throughout the stadium, in all the stands, named mainly after club legends

**Directions:**

**Air:** Liverpool and Manchester airports are both in 30 minutes travel from the stadium.

**Rail or bus:** St Helens Central rail station is only a five minute walk from the stadium. A new footbridge over the link way to the north of the stadium can be reached by following Shaw Street and then Chalon Way East.

**Road:** Exit Junction 7 from the M62; follow the A570 (St Helens Linkway) until Sherdley Road. Then bear left onto Peasley Cross Lane.

**Parking:** No public parking at ground, but three major car parks nearby for £1 a car. Park in the town centre and walk to the ground, 15 minutes.

## Salford City Reds

**Ground:** Salford City Stadium
**Address:** 1 Stadium Way, Eccles M30 7EY
**Phone:** 0161 820 2738
**Website:** www.reds.co.uk
**E-mail:** info@reds.co.uk
**Colours:** Red
**Capacity:** 12,000. **Seats:** 7,000. **Standing:** 5,000

**Club history:** Salford's nickname, The Red Devils, comes from a 1934 tour to France when the press described them as playing like devils, dubbing them Les Diables Rouges.
The club was founded in 1873 by the boys of the Cavendish Street Chapel in Hulme, Manchester. Using a local field, the boys organised matches among themselves before moving to nearby Moss Side. In an attempt to recruit new members, the link with the school was broken in 1875 and the name Cavendish Football Club was adopted. Cavendish became Salford Football Club in 1879. The first home match at New Barnes was a draw against Widnes on 11 October 1879. When the Northern Union was formed in 1895, Salford initially remained loyal to the Rugby Football Union, but in April 1896 the club held a special meeting to discuss joining the new organisation. Salford were admitted to the Northern Union on June 3 1896, with their first competitive match a 10-0 loss at Widnes. In the 1960s and early 1970s the club had a very successful period.
In January 2013 the hearing of a winding-up petition over money Salford owed to HM Revenue & Customs and to players in unpaid wages was adjourned so that new investors in the club could be sought. The club was then taken over by Doctor Marwan Koukash early in 2013.

**Stadium history:** From 1901 until the end of the 2011 season, Salford City Reds played their home games at The Willows, a small mainly terraced stadium with two stands. The capacity was 11,363 with only 2,500 seats. From the start of the 2012 season, the Reds have played at the purpose-built City of Salford Stadium in Barton-upon-Irwell, co-owned by Peel Holdings and Salford City Council and shared with rugby union side Sale Sharks. The ownership of the stadium may change in the future.

**The stadium:** The City of Salford Community Stadium has been built to hold 12,000, but there are plans to increase this to 20,000 'over time'. There are four stands: West (main) Stand: capacity 4,500; North (BMI Healthcare) Stand: all standing, capacity 2,500, usually the away end; East Stand: all-seater, capacity 2,500; South (Wellsprings) Stand: all standing, capacity 2,500, home fans.
**Ticket office:** 0844 8880 200. www.reds.co.uk/tickets

**Ticket prices: South, North and East stands: Pre-match purchase:** adult: £20; concessions: £15; under-16: £10; family: £40.
**West stand:** adult: £23; concession: £18, under-16: £13; family: £46.
For purchase on the day add £2.
Purchase on the day is at the ticket office for the stand.

**Supporters with disabilities:** Contact Elaine Bowers on 0161 736 6564 or 0161 820 2610. There is a club car park with 640 spaces for home and away supporters, split 70%/30% in favour of home supporters. The car park is 120 metres away from the accessible seating area in the West Car Park.
Home supporters have 61 spaces for wheelchair users available to them, and these can be found on an elevated platform (27 West Stand Hospitality) and pitch side (14 West Stand and 21 South Stand).
35 spaces for wheelchair users can be found at pitch side (15 North Stand) and on an elevated platform (20 East Stand) in the away section.
PA seats are found adjacent. Ambulant disabled seating is found throughout the East and West Stands.
Both home and away fans can use accessible toilets inside the stadium.
Catering kiosks in the home and away sections are accessible.
The stadium has a hearing loop at reception and in the West Stand. Match commentaries are available in all areas via the wire-free device.
Assistance dogs are welcome.

**Club shop:** There is a shop at the ground, and also online via the club website.

**Refreshments:** There are catering kiosks at the ground, and the club also offers match day hospitality facilities.

**Directions:**

**Rail:** Nearest stations are Irlam and Patricroft. From both stations walk to Liverpool Road and take the number 67 bus.

**Trams:** Nearest station is Eccles. From here the stadium is approximately 40 minutes walk or take the No 67 bus along Liverpool Road.
www.metrolink.co.uk

**Bus:** Bus from Manchester city centre and Eccles, number 67 to Liverpool Road, Irlam, then a two minute walk to the stadium
Bus from the Trafford Centre (Many services connect here from across the region), number 100 to Liverpool Road, Irlam.
Walk and Ride from The Willows: £1 per person, every 20 minutes.
The bus stop is a "two-minute walk" from the stadium according to the club website. It has also been described as "an eight minute brisk march".
www.tfgm.com 0871 200 22 33

**Road:** The stadium is located at Barton, close to Junction 11 of the M60 on the A57  Liverpool Road
N.B. Until the stadium postcode becomes operational on sat nav devices, use the postcode - M30 7LJ

Situated a few hundred yards from the M60, which is itself five minutes from the M62 the City of Salford Stadium would appear to be ideally placed. But there are no signs to the ground, and it is served by one single-carriage road in and out.

**Parking at Ground:** 600 parking spaces close to the stadium (pre-purchased at £5 per vehicle at the stadium or through Ticketline up until 10pm night before game), including accessible disabled parking, as well as coach parking. Overflow car parking available at City Airport and Heliport, less than 10 minutes walk from stadium.

**Parking nearby** There are a few dozen parking spots off the access road, but the rest are directed towards Barton airfield a few hundred yards further west. Parking is residents only along Liverpool Road.

**Park/Walk and Ride:** The cheapest and easiest way to get to the Stadium is by using the park and ride service. All services are direct and cost £1 per journey. The pick-up point is at the Trafford Centre. Buses will leave from the Event City car park near Barton Square.

## Sheffield Eagles

**Grounds:** The Eagles play the majority of their games at the Don Valley Stadium, but also play a number at Bramall Lane, the home of Sheffield United FC.

**Address:** Don Valley Stadium, Worksop Road, Sheffield S9 3TL
**Phone:** 0114 261 0326
**Fax:** 0114 261 0303
**Website:** www.sheffieldeagles.com
**E-mail:** info@sheffieldeagles.com
**Twitter:** @SheffieldEagles
**Colours:** White and red
**Capacity:** 25,000 (All seated)

**Club history:** In 1982 Huddersfield captain and chairman of the Players' Union, Gary Hetherington, missed out on a coaching job at York. So he decided to form his own club based in Sheffield. The club joined the Second Division in 1984 and played at the Owlerton Stadium. A competition was run in the *Sheffield Star* to find a name for the new club and "Sheffield Eagles" was the winner. The first Eagles league game was on September 2 1984 when they beat Rochdale Hornets 29–10. The Eagles record attendance was set in August 1997 when 10,603 fans saw them play Bradford Bulls.

**The stadium:** The Don Valley Stadium was opened in 1990 to host the 1991 World Student Games. It continues to be a major athletics arena, and is the second largest athletics stadium in the UK, behind only the London Olympic Stadium. The stadium's focal point is its 10,000 seat grandstand. A further 15,000 can be accommodated on the open terracing. It became the principal home of Sheffield Eagles in 1991. Don Valley is primarily an athletics stadium. Only the main stand is used for Eagles games, and so they can lack atmosphere due to the distance from the pitch and many empty seats. Its future is in doubt, because the local council has said it will not be funded after September 2013, and will probably close unless other funding or ownership is found. However, there are plans to use the site as part of a larger sports complex, including a new rugby stadium.

**Ticket office:** 0114 261 0326 or online: www.sheffieldeagles.com

**Ticket prices:** adult: £15; concessions: £10; student and junior: £5.

**Supporters with disabilities:** Designated area in main stand. Disabled toilets in main concourse near shop. Designated car parking at ground.

**Club shop:** Kiosk on stadium concourse, open on matchdays. Also from club offices: Monday to Friday: 9am to 4.30pm. Also online via club website.

**Refreshments:** Two kiosks on stadium concourse. Matchday hospitality packages available.

**Directions:**

**Don Valley**

**Rail:** Both Sheffield and Meadowhall Train Stations have connecting transport links to the stadium.

**Tram:** Sheffield's light-rail system has a dedicated stop within 100 metres of the stadium: Arena/Don Valley Stadium. Trams connect to the stadium from various locations in the city, including the City Centre & Meadowhall.

**Bus:** 69 bus for the stadium from Sheffield and Rotherham Transport Interchanges. www.travelsouthyorkshire.com

**Car:** Leave the M1 at junction 34 (Sheffield Meadowhall). At roundabout follow signs A6178 City Centre & Attercliffe. Go past Meadowhall Shopping Centre on the right. Keep straight on this road. Follow local signs to Attercliffe & Don Valley Stadium and Sheffield Arena. Go past the stadium to traffic lights and turn left. The VIP entrance and stadium car park is the second road on the left.

**Parking:** Parking at ground for VIP and disabled only. Coleridge Road car park available, street parking is limited.

**Bramall Lane**

The ground originally opened as a cricket ground in 1855, but the first football match was not played there until December 1862, when Sheffield FC played there, who are widely recognised as the oldest club in the world, being formed in 1857. This makes Bramall Lane the oldest professional football ground in the world. Now home to Sheffield United FC.

**Address:** Bramall Lane, Sheffield S2 4SU
**Capacity:** 32,072 (all seated)

**Ticket office:** The match day ticket office at Bramall Lane is based at the Executive Suites Entrance on John Street with the Malta Family Stand which is the stand used for Eagles matches.

**Directions:**

**Rail:** The ground is a one-mile walk from Sheffield Railway Station. Leave the station and turn left. At the Sheaf Street roundabout continue straight onto Suffolk Street. At the Granville Square roundabout turn right onto St Mary's Road. Take the second left into Shoreham Street and the ground is on the right.

**Tram and bus:** The ground is approximately a 10-minute walk from Granville Road (Sheffield College) tram stop. This stop is served by the Blue and Purple routes from the city centre bound for Halfway and Herdings Park respectively. Bus: Traveline: 01709 51 51 51

**Road:**

**From the M1 travelling south:** Exit the M1 at junction 33, following signs to Sheffield (A57). Continue along the Sheffield Parkway until the Park Square roundabout. Take the third exit and follow the A61 Sheaf Street, Sheffield Railway Station is on the left. At the Sheaf Street roundabout continue straight onto Suffolk Street. At the Granville Square roundabout turn right onto St Mary's Road. Take the second left into Shoreham Street and the ground is on the right.

**From the M1 travelling north:** Exit the M1 at Junction 29 and take the A617 towards Chesterfield. Continue into Chesterfield and at the roundabout junction with the A61 take the third exit towards Sheffield. Continue on the A61 through Dronfield and into Sheffield. Continue past the Earl of Arundel and Surrey public house on the left. Take the next left onto Bramall Lane and the ground is on the right.

**From the West:** Take the A57 into Sheffield and take the fourth exit at roundabout into Upper Hannover Street and at the second roundabout take the third exit into Bramall Lane.

**From the East:** Exit the M1 at junction 31 or 33, and take the A57 to the roundabout. Take the third exit and follow the A61 Sheaf Street, Sheffield Railway Station is on your left. At the Sheaf Street roundabout continue straight onto Suffolk Street. At the Granville Square roundabout turn right onto St Mary's Road. Take the second left into Shoreham Street and the ground is on the right.

**Off-street parking:**
Atkinsons: Charter Row: S1 4HR; Eyre Street, S1 4QW; Furnival Gate, Matilda way, S1 4QJ; Rockingham Way, S1 4JD; Sidney Street S1 4EG

## South Wales Scorpions

**Ground:** The John Smith's Gnoll
**Address:** Gnoll Park Road, Neath SA11 3BU.
**Office address:** South Wales Scorpions RLFC, Floor 1, 13, Old Market Street, Neath, Wales SA11 3NA.
**Phone:** 01639 636 585
**Website:** www.scorpionsrl.com
**E-mail:** info@scorpionsrl.com
**Twitter:** @ScorpionsRugbyL
**Colours:** Home: pink shirts with black trim. Away: yellow
**Capacity:** 5,000

**Stadium history:** South Wales Scorpions were formed in 2009, after the Crusaders left South Wales and moved to Wrexham in North Wales. They are the only professional rugby league side in South Wales and have played at the Gnoll since their formation. The Gnoll is the traditional home of Neath RFC. It has also been home to association football – Welsh Premier League club Neath Athletic played there between 2008 and their liquidation in 2012 – and even first-class cricket.

**Ticket prices:** adults: £12; concessions: £7; juniors: £3.

**Supporters with disabilities:** Contact: Ian Golden on 01639 636 585 or 07830 109093 There is a public car park 100 metres away with accessible parking spaces. There are 6 accessible seats for wheelchair users split 50/50 with away fans. All are undercover with unobstructed views.
Catering facilities are accessible. The Family stand has an accessible toilet. If seated in the Main Stand accessible toilet facilities are available in the club house. Assistance dogs are welcome.

**Club Shop:** www.scorpionsrl.com/shop and at 13 Old Market Street, Neath SA11 3NA.

**Refreshments:** There are a number of food and drink outlets at The Gnoll. There are outdoor bars and food outlets at the opposite end of the ground including Calve's Corner that also sell confectionary.

**Directions**

**Rail** Neath station is a 10 minute walk from The Gnoll. There are direct trains from London, Cardiff and Swansea to Neath and local services.

**Road:** Exit the M4 at junction 43 and follow the A465 into the town. At the roundabout follow the signs to Cimla and Pontrhydyfen. At the traffic lights go straight ahead until approaching a second roundabout. The Gnoll is directly ahead.

**Parking:** There are two public car parks almost opposite the ground.

## Swinton Lions

**Ground:** Leigh Sports Village
**Club office:** 105-107 Chorley Road, Swinton, Manchester M27 4AA
**Phone:** 0161 794 6150
**Fax:** 0161 425 1052
**Website:** www.swintonlionsrlc.co.uk
**E-mail:** info@swintonlionsrlc.co.uk
**Twitter:** @swintonlion
**Colours** Blue & White
**Capacity:** 11,000

**Stadium history:** The club was formed in 1866 when members of Swinton Cricket Club decided to take up football in the winter. In 1871 they joined the Rugby Football Union under the name Swinton and Pendlebury FC. As a rugby league club they have won the Championship six times and three Challenge Cups. From 1929 until 1992 they played at their famous Station Road ground in Swinton. But the ground was sold for housing to pay off debts, and the club moved to share Bury FC's Gigg Lane ground. The club lost a layer of support through this move, and left Gigg Lane in 2002. They are currently planning to build a new ground in Swinton.
They are currently ground-sharing at Leigh Sports Village, which is covered in the Leigh Centurions section.

**Ticket Office:** Tickets are available from Leigh Sports Village and the Leigh Sports Village website, as well as the club office from Thursday and Friday morning 10am to 4.30pm.

**Ticket prices:** adults: £15, concessions: £10; junior: £5.

**Supporters with disabilities:** Contact Trevor Barton on 07973 116985. See Leigh Centurions entry for details

**Club shop:** Items can be purchased online via the club's website.

**Catering:** See Leigh Centurions entry for details. There are hospitality packages available – see the club website for details.

**Directions:** See Leigh Centurions entry for details

**Parking at ground:** There is plenty of onsite parking.

## University of Gloucestershire All Golds

**Ground:** Prince of Wales Stadium
**Address:** Tommy Taylors Lane, Cheltenham, Gloucestershire GL50 4NJ
**Office:** Oxstalls Campus, Gloucester GL2 9HW
**Phone** 01242 715332
**Website:** www.allgoldsrugby.com
**E-mail:** rwebber@glos.ac.uk
**Twitter:** @AllGolds
**Colours:** Light blue and dark blue
**Capacity:** 490 seated plus standing room by running track.

**Stadium history:** Rugby league at the University started in 1996. In March 2013 the University of Gloucestershire All Golds entered the semi-professional ranks joining Championship 1. The Prince of Wales Stadium is a multi-sport stadium which opened in 1981. It is also home to Cheltenham Tigers rugby union club and Cheltenham & County Harriers. The 1907–08 New Zealand tourists played the Northern Union in the town; hence the team name 'All Golds'.

**The stadium:** The stadium has a covered stand with 490 seats, and is linked to a recreation centre on the same site.

**Ticket prices:** adults: £10; concessions: £6; under-16: free with an adult.

**Supporters with disabilities:** Disabled toilet near main entrance, contact club for advice and information before attending a match.

**Club shop:** Online via club website, no matchday facilities yet.

**Refreshments:** Bar (go out of main entrance, turn left & left upstairs) serves drinks, tea & coffee and some snacks. Roast pork and spare ribs stall by stand.

**Directions:**

**Rail:** Cheltenham Spa station. www.firstgreatwestern.co.uk

**Bus:** Cheltenham, Royal Well for coaches. Buses: www.travellinesw.com

**Road:** The ground is north of the town centre, near the racecourse. From the A40 from Oxford, after junction with A435, turn right into Hales Road, which leads into Priors Road, fork right into Bouncers Lane. Turn left at mini-roundabouts and right into Tatchley Lane. Pass racecourse, go straight over roundabout into Swindon Lane, turn left at mini-roundabout into Tommy Taylor Lane. Ground on the right. (Route not suitable for coaches) From the M5, exit at Junction 11 and take the A40 into Cheltenham, then follow signs for 'The Recreation Centre'.

**Parking:** At ground or leisure centre across the road.

The stand at The Prince of Wales Stadium, home of the University of Gloucestershire All Golds.

All Golds versus Oxford at the Prince of Wales Stadium, March 2013.

## Wakefield Trinity Wildcats

**Ground:** The Rapid Solicitors Stadium (Belle Vue)
**Address:** Doncaster Road, Wakefield WF1 5EY
**Phone:** 01924 211 611
**Fax:** 01924 211765
**Website:** www.wakefieldwildcats.co.uk
**E-mail:** info@wakefieldwildcats.co.uk
**Twitter:** @WTWildcatsRL
**Colours:** Home: white; away: blue
**Capacity:** 12,600.

**Club history:** Wakefield Trinity is one of the original 22 rugby clubs that formed the Northern Union in 1895. They are one of the sport's great historical clubs, and were one of the leading clubs in the 1960s, winning the Challenge Cup and the Championship.

**Stadium history:** The site was purchased in 1895 after the spilt to provide a permanent base for Wakefield Trinity. Belle Vue was the venue for the 1923 Challenge Cup Final, in which Leeds beat Hull 28–3 in front of 29,335, the only occasion on which the ground was so honoured.
Many scenes from the film *This Sporting Life* were filmed at the Belle Vue Stadium during Wakefield's third round Challenge Cup match against Wigan in 1962.
The capacity of the stadium was increased to 12,000 in 2008. The Wildcats have long been in negotiation with the local council to find an alternative site, as the present stadium does not comply with Super League standards. Plans for a 12,000 seater stadium near junction 30 of the M62, in Stanley, were unveiled in April 2009, but in December 2010 the Secretary of State ruled that the application should be referred, meaning a substantial delay. So, in June 2011 the club announced that it would redevelop the existing ground to a capacity of 12,000. Cover has now been added to the open terrace behind the goal. In 2012, the government finally granted planning permission for a new community stadium that will be used by the Wildcats. The hope is this will be ready for the 2015 season.

**The stadium:** Currently, the East Stand has a covered stand with seating, with some terracing in front. The North and West sides are terraces, with cover behind the goal. The South side is the location of hospitality facilities. Someone once wrote: "If Alice in Wonderland designed a rugby league ground it would look something like this. There are hatches, doorways and steps everywhere. Every hatch is serving a different food and/or beer, every doorway leads to a toilet, and look through any window and its likely to be a very busy bar with no obvious entrance."
Belle Vue is one of only four grounds that have survived since 1895. The Western terrace is designated for away fans, turnstiles 21 and 22.

**Ticket office:** Tickets can be pre-purchased from the Wildcats retail outlet in the Ridings Shopping Centre or at the Rapid Solicitors Stadium Box Office. Tickets also by calling 01924 201548, or via the club's website.

**Ticket prices: Standing:** adult: £20 in advance, £22 match day; concessions (5 to 16 year olds and over 60): £12; under 5s free.
**Seating: East Stand wing:** adult: £21, £23 match day; concessions: £13.
**Seating: East Stand centre:** adults: £22, £24 match day; concessions: £17. To sit in the East Stand wing or centre, buy tickets in advance. You will not be able to pay on the day. With a ground standing ticket, there is a £1 upgrade fee to sit in the East Stand wing and a £2 upgrade fee for the East Stand centre.

**Supporters with disabilities:** Contact Davide Longo on 07894 585 466. There are up to 20 accessible parking spaces, with up to five for away supporters. Prior booking required
There are 15 accessible seats for home fans and five for away fans in the East Stand at pitch side. Carers sit adjacent.
There is a waitress service that caters for the needs of disabled supporters. The accessible toilets are behind the East Stand and behind the pitch side area. The club offers an audio descriptive commentary service, with five headsets in the East Stand. Assistance dogs are welcome.

**Club shop:** www.wakefieldwildcats.co.uk/store
There is an outlet in the Ridings Shopping Centre and a shop at the ground.

**Refreshments:** The Trinity Bar is on the bottom floor of the hospitality suite within the ground, with a balcony view over the pitch and Wakefield memorabilia adorning the walls. The CATS Bar is just outside the main entrance. There are other refreshment stalls in the ground, and hospitality packages available.

**Local refreshments:** Just outside the city centre is the Cathedral Retail Park. There are the usual range of fast food outlets, together with a Pizza Hut, a Nando's and a Frankie & Bennys.

**Directions:**

**Rail:** Trains from Leeds, Sheffield, Doncaster and York go into Westgate Station. Trains from Barnsley, Huddersfield, Goole, Castleford and Featherstone go into Kirkgate Station. Sandal & Agbrigg Station is the nearest to the stadium, located about half a mile from the ground.

**Bus:** The following buses serve the stadium: 105,106,122,123, 145,148, 149,150, 167,168, 172,182, 184,185, 189,192, 193, 485, 489, 497, 498. www.arrivabus.co.uk

**Road:**

**From the M1:** Take junction 39, take the A636 Denby Dale Road towards Wakefield**.** At the first roundabout (Asdale Road) carry straight on towards the city, where you will see the Campanile Hotel on the left.
Bear right under the railway bridge and continue towards the city, with Wakefield Park on the left. Go straight across the min-roundabout and under the arches, take a right at the next roundabout and head along Ings Road with Sainsbury and Homebase on the right.
Follow the signs for the A638 Doncaster Road. Once on Doncaster Road the ground is on the right after about half a mile.

**From the M62:** Take junction 31 and take the A655 towards Wakefield. Turn right onto the A638, go under the railway bridges. Head straight on and the Superbowl is on the left. The Stadium is just beyond on the left.

**Parking:** There are parking spaces on local streets. However, street parking is restricted, including some match day restrictions. A popular spot is on Sugar Lane near to the cemetery, but places get taken quickly.
There are quite a few car parks in Wakefield city centre, with a 15 minute walk to the ground. Another option is Denmark Street, a few minutes walk north of the ground.

## Warrington Wolves

**Ground:** The Halliwell Jones Stadium
**Address:** Mike Gregory Way, Warrington, Cheshire, WA2 7NE
**Phone:** 01925 248880
**Fax:** 01925 248899
**Website:** www.warringtonwolves.com
**E-mail:** info@warringtonwolves.com
**Twitter:** @wolvesrl
**Colours:** Home: white, with blue trimmings; away: black.
**Capacity:** 15,200.

**Club history:** Warrington are one of the 22 clubs that formed the Northern Union in 1895, and has played every season in the top flight. In 1974 they won four cups, but their last Championship win was in 1955.

**Stadium history:** By the late 1990s Warrington's spiritual home, Wilderspool Stadium, had become unfit for purpose, and the club decided to move to a new stadium. The last Warrington competitive game at Wilderspool, was on 21 September 2003, when Warrington beat Wakefield Trinity Wildcats 52–12. Warrington then moved to the Halliwell Jones Stadium in 2003. Planning permission for the new stadium had been granted in 2001, and it was built in conjunction with Tescos. A Tesco Extra store is located on the north of the site. Halliwell Jones is a north-west based motor group. The first game at the stadium was on 21 February 2004. Warrington beat Wakefield Trinity Wildcats 34–20.

**The stadium:** The stadium is notable for bucking the common trend of modern stadia building by including terracing rather than being all-seater. There are four stands: the North Stand (reserved seating), the East Stand (originally unreserved seating, but later became reserved seating), the South Stand (home terracing) and the West Stand (visitors terracing and overflow of home terracing). It also has enormous pitch dimensions of 120m x 74m, as requested by Warrington's then head coach Paul Cullen, due to his desire to play expansive rugby. The stadium capacity, set at 15,000 for the first sell-out home match against St Helens in 2012, was increased to 15,200. The club has also announced plans to increase the capacity to 18,000.

**Ticket prices:** First price is pre-match day; match day in brackets
**Seating** (Blocks I-Q) formerly North: adult: £27.50 (£29.00); concession (60+, student, 16-18 young adult, junior): £18.50 (£20); infant (under-5): free (£20).
**Seating** (Blocks A-H) formerly East and Quadrant: adult: £22.00 (£23.50); concession: £14.00 (£15.50); infant: free (£15.50)
**Standing:** adult: £19.00 (£20.00); concession: £13.00 (£14.00); infant: free (£14.00).

**Supporters with disabilities:** Contact: Bernie Lenihan 01925 248 880 or 07930 958383. There are 28 parking spaces for home supporters and four for away supporters. Home supporters have 13 accessible spaces for wheelchair users on high level platforms – 84 feet above ground level. Away supporters have 22 at ground level – front row accessible places for wheelchair users. Carers sit adjacent. All kiosks are fully accessible and accessible toilets are located near accessible seating. The club has a hearing loop and offers audio commentary, though this needs to be pre-booked.

**Refreshments:** There are refreshment bars and food stalls throughout the stadium with a wide variety of food and drinks. There are also pre-match meals and hospitality packages available.

**Club shop:** Items can be purchased online via the club website, and there is also a shop at the ground, near the main entrance.

**Directions**

**Rail:** The nearest station to the stadium is Warrington Central. From the station, turn right and the Martin Dawes East Stand is visible. Continue along this road to the stadium. Warrington Bank Quay Station is just over a mile from the stadium. A taxi should take no more than five minutes.

**Bus:** Warrington Bus Station is a short distance from the Stadium, near to Central train Station. Exit the station and turn left down Winwick Street and past Central station on the right. Continue towards the Stadium. www.warringtonboroughtransport.co.uk

**Road:**

**From the North:** Take junction 9 off the M62 and head south towards Warrington along the A49. After 1.5 miles, go straight on through the lights, with McDonalds on the right. Proceed past the Tesco Superstore and the Halliwell Jones Stadium before turning right at the next set of traffic lights. At the small roundabout take the first exit on to Winwick Street and there is the entrance to the NCP Car Park 50 yards further on, on the right hand side. The stadium is immediately across from the Tesco store.

**From the South:** Leave M6 at Junction 21 and follow the A57 towards Warrington until the Cockhedge roundabout. Take the exit signposted A49 Wigan. Turn left at the next set of lights onto Pinners Brow. At the circle take the first exit on to Winwick Street and there is the entrance to the NCP Car Park 50 yards further on, on the right. The stadium is immediately across from the Tesco store.

**Parking:** Do not park in the Tesco car park on a matchday without a valid pass and use the designated area. Tesco will issue £50 fines. If you enter the Tesco Car Park from the A49 in error, take the exit back out and turn left onto the A49 heading north, then follow the "Directions from the South."

# Warrington Wolves: The Halliwell Jones Stadium

History at Warrington's Halliwell Jones stadium: Jack Fish remembered on the left, the Brian Bevan statue on the right.

A full terrace watches the Wolves play Salford in May 2012.

## Whitehaven

**Ground:** The Recreation Ground (The 'Recre')
**Address:** Coach Road, Whitehaven, Cumbria CA28 9DD.
**Phone:** 01946 328 088
**Website:** www.whitehavenrl.co.uk
**E-mail:** info@whitehaverl.co.uk
**Twitter:** @Whitehaven_Rlfc
**Colours:** White, Blue and Yellow
**Capacity:** 7,500. **Seats:** 556. **Standing:** 6,944.

**Stadium history:** The Recreation Ground was originally the playing fields for local miners and was owned by the Miners Welfare organisation. It opened in 1933 as an enclosed field with one wooden stand. The ground in its current form was built in 1948 to enable the newly-formed Whitehaven to play in the Rugby Football League. The link with the Miners Welfare poses a potential brake on any outside investment in the ground.

**The stadium:** The ground now has terracing on three sides, with one end, the Kells End, covered. The other sides are known as the Popular Side, the Railway End, and the LLWR Repository Stand, which seats 556. The stadium is due to have a second seated stand holding 1,100 where the Popular Side terracing now stands.

**Ticket prices:** LLWR Repository Stand (seated): adult: £15; concessions: £10; under-16s: £5. Seating is unreserved. Rest of the ground (standing): adult: £15; concessions: £10; under-16s: £5.

**Club shop:** Merchandise available online via the club website, or from: Whitehaven Embroidery, Queen Street, Whitehaven CA28 7QF. Tel: 01946 590952. Email enquiries: merchandise@whitehavenrl.co.uk

**Refreshments:** Pre-match hospitality available in the Garry Purdham Lounge, drinks in the JJ McKeowen Bar and food available in the ground.

**Directions**

**Rail:** Change to the Whitehaven line at Carlisle. Get off at the second Whitehaven stop, Corkickle. The stadium is a five minute walk from the ground.

**Road:**
From the North-East: A69 to Carlisle, then the A595 towards Cockermouth and then onwards towards Whitehaven.
From Lancashire and the South: M6 to the Penrith interchange (signposted North Lakes) and then take the A66 to Keswick and towards Workington, turning left onto the A595 after Cockermouth.

**Parking:** Local street parking available and some at the ground.

## Widnes Vikings

**Ground:** Stobart Stadium Halton.
**Address:** Lowerhouse Lane, Widnes, Cheshire WA8 7DZ.
**Phone:** 0151 495 2250
**Fax:**
**Website:** www.widnesvikings.co.uk
**E-mail:** enquiries@widnesvikings.co.uk
**Colours:** Black and White

**Capacity:** 13,500 (all seated)

**Club history:** Widnes were one of the original clubs that formed the Northern Union in 1895. Before Super League they were one of the strongest teams in British rugby league, and were dubbed the 'Cup Kings' after going to Wembley almost every year in the late 1970s and early 1980s. They were not originally in Super League, and after a spell of consolidation in November 2007 the club was bought by Steve O'Connor, a local businessman. By 2011 the club had regained Super League status.

**Stadium history:** Widnes RLFC settled at Lowerhouse Lane in 1895. The death of the club's secretary, Tom Naughton, in 1932, led to the ground being renamed Naughton Park. It was agreed with Halton Council that a new stadium would be built on the existing site, and it was officially opened on November 2, 1997. The stadium reached completion with the opening of the East Stand in September 2005, and was renamed the Stobart Stadium Halton in December 2007.

**Ticket office:** Vikings Store ticket Hotline: 0151 422 8383

**Ticket prices:** Advance ticket prices (Match day prices in brackets)
**North and South Stands:** adult: £20 (£22); concession: £13 (£15); junior: £11 (£13).
**South Stand Silver (via main reception):** adult: £28 (£30); concession: £20 (£22); junior: £14 (£16).
**South Stand Gold (via main reception):** £40 standard price

Buy tickets from the ticket office before entering the ground, because the stadium does not operate cash turnstiles. Concessions: 65 and over, or full-time students aged over 16, proof required.

Away fans use the East Stand, tickets can be purchased at the turnstiles.

**Supporters with disabilities:** Contact Janet Pheysey on 0151 495 2250. There are 15 accessible parking spaces for home fans, and six for away supporters, located behind the East Stand. There are 21 accessible spaces in the North and South Stands for home supporters and 16 accessible places in the East and West Stands for away supporters. All are covered but are at pitch side. There is easy access to toilets and refreshment areas.

The club has an induction loop. Assistance dogs are welcome in the North and South Stands with prior notification.
Supporters with disabilities pay for their tickets at the appropriate price, a carer can enter free, but must accompany the supporter to the ticket office and have appropriate ID.

**Club shop:** Items can be ordered online, and there is a Vikings merchandise store in the local Tesco Extra store. Opening hours: Monday 9am to 5pm, Tuesday to Friday 11am to 7pm, Saturday 9am to 5pm, Sunday 11am to 5pm. Items are also available from O'Neill's via the club website.

**Refreshments:** The concourses in all four stands are well equipped with bars, where food and drink is served. There are also vending machines. There is a McDonalds about five minutes walk from the stadium, and a KFC about a 10 minute walk the other way.
The Cricketers Arms is located at the south-west corner of the ground. Match day meals and hospitality packages available.

**Directions:**

**Rail and Bus:** The town is served by Widnes Railway Station, and a bus service runs from there to the town centre.

**Road:**

**From the North, via M62:** Take Junction 7 and then A568 dual carriageway towards Widnes following brown signs to Halton Stadium. Take Ashley Way (A562) and then second exit of roundabout (McDonalds on the right) and second exit off mini-roundabout into Lowerhouse Lane.

**From Runcorn and the South:** Cross Widnes/Runcorn Bridge (A533). Take signs to Widnes (A562). At roundabout take third exit towards Widnes Town Centre and first left following brown signs to Halton Stadium (McDonalds on the right) and 2nd exit off mini-roundabout into Lowerhouse Lane.

**From south Liverpool:** Take Speke Road (A562) and follow signs to Widnes. Continue following brown signs to Halton Stadium. Take first exit off next roundabout (McDonalds on the right) and second exit off mini-roundabout into Lowerhouse Lane.

**Parking at ground:** Widnes Vikings cannot offer entry to its on-site car park for spectators on match days.
However, the Municipal Car Park on Caldwell Road is only a five minute walk from the stadium and offers free parking as an added bonus.

The ground is surrounded by a housing estate, although any spaces can be taken quickly. The town centre isn't far from the ground.

## Wigan Warriors

**Ground:** DW Stadium
**Stadium address:** Loire Drive, Robin Park, Wigan WN5 0UH
Club offices: Central Park, Montrose Avenue, Wigan WN5 9XL
**Phone:** 01942 762888
**Fax:** 01942 762889
**Website:** www.wiganwarriors.com
**E-mail:** info@wiganwarriors.com
**Twitter:** @WiganWarriorsRL
**Colours:** Home: cherry and white hoops, white shorts, cherry and white hooped socks. Away: black, with gold trim.
**Capacity:** 25,168 (all seated)

**Club history:** On November 21 1872, Wigan Football Club was founded by members of Wigan Cricket Club, following a meeting at the Royal Hotel, Standishgate. Their first competitive match was a draw against Warrington on 18 January 1873. Wigan were founder members of the Northern Union in 1895. Wigan are the most successful club in the history of British rugby league, having won 19 league championships (including two Super League Grand Final victories), 18 Challenge Cups and three World Club Challenge trophies. They had a period of sustained success from the mid-1980s to the mid-1990s, winning the Challenge Cup eight seasons in succession and the league championship seven seasons in succession. Since moving to their new stadium, Wigan Warriors' success has not been as high as it was at Central Park. However, in 2011 they won the Challenge Cup, and after a poor period are now once again one of the game's leading clubs.

**Stadium history:** In 1902 Wigan moved to their purpose-built rugby ground, Central Park. This was the home of Wigan Rugby League until 1999, when they moved to the newly-built JJB Stadium, now re-named the DW Stadium. The first game at the JJB Stadium was a Super-League play-off match against Castleford Tigers, which Wigan lost 14-10.
The DW Stadium is shared with Wigan Athletic Football Club: the football club are to become owners but as a guarantee to Wigan Rugby League, the rugby club was given a 50-year lease on the stadium.

**The stadium:** The DW Stadium was opened in 1999. The four stands are roughly the same height and there is an electric scoreboard above the Boston (East) Stand, on one side of the stadium. The stadium is not totally enclosed, all corners being open. There is plenty of leg room between the rows of seats and the views of the pitch are excellent. The stands seem to rise up quite steeply and do sit back a fair distance from the pitch.
Being a modern stadium, an atmosphere is usually difficult to create unless it is fairly full – which it isn't always.
The North Stand is used for away fans. Situated behind the posts, it holds

5,400. The East Stand (holding 8,238), known as the Boston Stand, and the western (Springfield Stand, holding 6,100) run across the longer sides of the pitch. The latter contains the stadium's "vital facilities". The un-named South Stand holds 5,412.

**Ticket Office:** The DW Stadium ticket office is located at the northerly end of the West Stand, and is open Monday to Friday between 9am and 5pm, and on Saturday mornings from 9am to midday.
On Warriors home match days the ticket office is open until kick-off, and for 15 minutes following the final hooter.
Ticket Hotline: 0871-6633552. Website: www.wiganwarriors.com/tickets

**Ticket prices:** West Stand (Gold): adult: £24; concession / junior: £18; West Stand (Blue): adult: £23; concession / junior: £17;
East Stand (Silver): adult: £22; concession / junior: £16; East Stand (Red): adult: £21; concession / junior: £15; South Stand: adult: £20; concession / junior: £14; North Stand (away): adult: £21; concession / junior: £15.
The East and West Stands have reserved seating, while the South Stand has unreserved seating. The North Stand is for visiting supporters.

**Supporters with disabilities:** Each stand at the DW Stadium has two designated disabled platforms in prime positions, with catering and toilet facilities available along with a lift to each concourse and direct access to the platforms. These platforms are designated for wheelchair users, with carers' seats alongside the platforms. Additional facilities for wheelchair users and supporters with other disabilities are available in front of the West Stand. Concessionary rates apply to disabled supporters. Should a carer be needed, admission is available at no extra charge at the discretion of the club. Match commentary facilities are available for visually impaired supporters in the West Stand. Headsets available, on payment of a refundable deposit of £15. The designated disability coordinator at the ticket office is Norma Sherratt. Phone: 0871-6633552

**Club shop:** There is a match day shop in the West Stand that is open two hours before kick-off, but not after the game. There is a shop in the town centre: Warriors World, Unit 40, Grand Arcade, Wigan WN1 1BH. (For sat nav use WN1 1YP). The nearby Waterstones and WH Smith branches both have a good selection of rugby league books. Phone: 01942-239655, or order via club website. E-mail: store@wiganwarriors.com

**Refreshments:** There are food and drink kiosks in the stadium. Hospitality packages available. There is a Pizza Hut and Frankie & Bennys close to the ground and a little further afield there are McDonalds and Burger King.

**Local refreshments:** The traditional pub for away fans is the Red Robin, which is only a few minutes walk away from the ground opposite the cinema complex. In the centre of town is a Wetherspoons outlet called the Moon under Water. Also worth a visit is the award-winning Anvil pub, next to the bus station. Both these pubs are listed in the *CAMRA Good Beer Guide.* Also there is the Berkeley on Wallgate, near the railway station. As at many grounds, it can take an age to get away by car, so maybe have a meal after the match in one of the nearby restaurants. Within 100 metres of the ground there is a Franky & Bennys, an Indian restaurant and many others.

**Directions:**

**Air:** Wigan is served by two international airports. Manchester Airport is a major international hub, serving most destinations across the world. It is 30 miles east of Wigan, and is accessible via the M6 and M56. Liverpool Airport is the north west base for many low-cost carriers, including RyanAir and EasyJet. It is located 32 miles west of Wigan, along the M58 and M57.

**Rail:** There are two train stations in Wigan, both next to each other in the town centre. Wigan Wallgate is on the Southport – Manchester Piccadilly line, and Wigan North Western is on the West Coast Mainline.
The stations are a good 20 minute walk from the ground. So either take a taxi, or break up the journey with a few pub stops along the way. On exiting Wigan North Western station, turn left and go down the road heading under a railway bridge.
On leaving Wallgate Station turn right and go down the road, passing Wigan North Western station on the left and then proceed under the railway bridge. It is a fairly straight walk along Robin Park Road. At the Seven Stars Hotel turn right and follow the locals on a shortcut along a canal to the stadium, or take the next road on the right.

**Road:**

**From the South**: Leave the M6 at junction 25, and take the A49 to Wigan. After around two miles there is an Aldi store on the left, before a large roundabout that is traffic light controlled. Turn left at this roundabout into Robin Park Road and continue into Scot Lane. The ground is down Scot Lane on your right.

**From the North**: Leave the M6 at Junction 26 and follow the signs for Wigan town centre – this road meets the A49 – turn left into Robin Park and continue into Scot Lane. The ground is down Scot Lane on the right.

**Parking:** There is a large car park at the stadium which costs £4 per car or motorbike, £10 for mini-buses, and £20 for coaches. There is sometimes quite a delay in getting out of this car park after the game. Do not park on the nearby Retail Park, as parking there is restricted to two hours and over-stayers may get parking tickets (£50).

# Workington Town

**Ground:** Derwent Park Stadium
**Address:** Workington CA14 2HG
**Phone:** 01900-603609
**Website:** www.townrlfc.com
**E-mail:** barry.scholey@townrlfc.co.uk
**Capacity:** 10,000. **Seats:** 1,200. **Standing:** 8,800

**Stadium history:** The stadium was opened in 1956. The record attendance was set in 1965 when 17,741 spectators turned up for a third round Challenge Cup match against Wigan. Before 1956, the club shared Workington AFC's adjoining ground.

**The stadium:** Workington Town share their ground with the speedway team Workington Comets. There is a large grandstand, and cover on the far side. However, the speedway track means that supporters are further from the pitch than at many stadiums.

**Ticket prices:** adult: £15 (grandstand), £14 (ground); concession: £10; under-16: £4; wheelchair user and carer £10.

**Supporters with disabilities:** Contact June Kennedy or M. Jackson on 01900-603609. There are 10 accessible car parking spaces with four for away supporters. These are located 100 metres from the entrance. Disabled viewing area has six spaces for wheelchair users, two are given to away supporters. This area is not under cover. The bars are located under the main grandstand. There are accessible catering facilities, and accessible toilets are 15 metres from the accessible seating area.

**Club shop:** Phone 01900 603 609 or email barry.scholey@townrlfc.co.uk Items can be ordered on line via the club's website. Commercial manager's office is a shop in the week, and in a cabin in the car park on matchdays.

**Refreshments:** The main bar at Derwent Park is the Gus Risman bar under the main stand. This bar is accessible from both within the ground and from the car park. The Rough & Ready bar is situated at the south end of the popular side stand. It opens 30 minutes before kick-off on match days only. Hot food is available from a catering van at the south end of the enclosure in front of the main stand. Match day hospitality packages available.

**Directions**

**Rail:** The ground is a short walk from Workington station.

**Road:** From the north, approach the town on A596. Turn right onto A597 (New Bridge Road). The ground is on right, just past Borough Park. From the south, approach on A597; turn right just past railway station, and ground is on left, next to Superstore. Parking at ground and in local streets.

## York City Knights

**Ground:** Huntington Stadium
**Address:** Roland Court, Huntington Road, York YO32 9PW
**Phone:** 01904 767404
**Website:** www.yorkcityknights.co.uk
**E-mail:** info@ycknights.co.uk
**Twitter:** @YorkKnightsRLFC
**Colours**: Home: dark blue; away: white, black and red.
**Capacity:** 3,428

**The stadium:** Huntington Stadium was formerly the Ryedale Stadium. It was completed in October 1989, and as it was financed by Ryedale District Council, so it was named Ryedale Stadium. It has facilities including a seated Main Stand incorporating executive boxes, a Popular Stand, floodlights, an electronic scoreboard and an athletics track. It has long been proposed that the Knights should share a new municipal stadium with York City FC, and it was announced in July 2010 that the preferred location would be the site of the current Huntington Stadium.
When conditions are dry supporters also gather on the grass banking to the right of the popular stand. The main turnstiles open one hour before kick-off; the turnstiles on Jockey Lane open 30 minutes before kick-off, for ticket holders only.

**Ticket prices:** Entry on match day: adults: £14; over 65s and students: £10; under-16s: £3. Transfer to seating: £2.

**Supporters with disabilities:** People with disabilities are charged concessionary rate of £10 or under-16s £5; carers / helpers will be charged full price. There are six wheelchair spaces (same level as pitch), and the best access is through the side gate near to the main turnstiles at the Courtneys (Nuffield) gym end of the ground. Toilets are located either opposite the main turnstiles next to the food kiosk or on the first floor of the bar area for wheelchair users.

**Club shop:** The club shop is situated in the corridor from the wooden staircase to Bar 13 (formerly box 1). Online shop via the club website.

**Refreshments:**
Bar 13: Supporters can access the bar via the staircase in main reception from 12:30pm. To enter the ground, go through the turnstiles which open at 2pm. There is no access from the bar to the stadium except for vice presidents, sponsors and guests with boardroom passes. There is a food kiosk run by the club opposite the main turnstiles, and a burger van. Hospitality boxes and packages available.

**Directions:**

**Rail:** York station is on the East Coast Main Line. The station is over 3 miles from the ground, and a taxi is probably the best way to get there.

**Road:** The stadium two miles north of the city centre, and very close to Monk's Cross Retail Park. It is off the A1036 (Malton Road), which is off the A1237 and A64. From the city centre take the A1036.

**From Harrogate and the A1 (North):** Follow the A59 sign posted York to the first roundabout. Turn left onto the A1237. Go straight and then follow the sign for Monks Cross Shopping Park.

**From Leeds and the A1 (South):** Follow the A64 sign posted York. Continue to follow the A64 to the first roundabout (approx 20 miles); turn left signposted York; turn left at the next roundabout (A1036 and Monks Cross South).

**Parking:** There are 180 car park spaces available on match days. This car park is located at the end of the main Courtney's / Waterworld car park and costs £3.

## 2. Catalan Dragons

**Ground:** Stade Gilbert Brutus
**Address:** 10 Avenue du Languedoc, 66000 Perpignan, France
**Phone:** 00 33 4683 53259
**Fax:** 00 33 4689 24860
**Website:** www.catalansdragons.com
**E-mail:** info@catalansdragons.com
**Colours:** Home: White; away: Orange
**Capacity:** 13,000.

**Club history:** The club was formed in 2000 by a merger of XIII Catalan and AS Saint Esteve into Union Treiziste Catalane (UTC). They won the 2005 French Rugby League Championship and the Lord Derby Cup in 2004 and 2005. In 2006 they were granted a Super League license, taking the name Catalan Dragons. UTC continues to compete in the French Championship's Elite One Championship as a feeder club for the Dragons.

**Stadium history:** During the 1970s and 1980s the Stade Gilbert Brutus was used by both league and union clubs in the area. Prior to 2007 the stadium could only hold 4,200, with only 900 seats. The first stage of construction involved the building of two covered, all-seater stands, and further construction has brought the capacity up to 13,000 with three all-seater stands. The Bonzoms Stand was renovated in 2007 and now has 3,000 'blood and gold' seats.

**Ticket office:** The Dragons have several sales outlets for match tickets. Tickets can be bought at the gate on match day, but also in advance:
At the Gilbert Brutus Stadium from the Wednesday prior to the match.
Tickets can also be bought through the 'Ticket Net' network at Auchan, Leclerc, Virgin Megastore, Cultura, Cora

**Ticket prices: Bonzoms Stand:** Official: 40 Euros; Gold: 30 Euros; Silver: 25 Euros. **Guasch Laborde:** Bronze: 25 Euros. **West Stand:** 18 Euros. **General admission:** Standing: 15 Euros. Student and concession standing: 10 Euros. Children standing: 3 Euros.

**Supporters with disabilities:** Contact Richet Lise: 33 4 68 35 32 59. There is no private parking for supporters with disabilities, but they can park near the stadium where there are disabled spaces. Disabled or ambulant fans will need to offer proof of their disability, in which case admission is free.
There are 18 home spaces for wheelchair users and nine for away. Carer is located next to wheelchair user. All toilets and refreshment areas are accessible to supporters with disabilities.

**Club shop:** Boutique des Dragons Catalans, Stade Gilbert Brutus

Avenue de l' Aerodrome, 66000 Perpignan. Phone: 00 33 4 68 63 83 74
Open: Wednesday to Saturday: 9 am to noon and 2 pm to 6 pm.
Also at 3rd floor, Galeries Lafayette Shop, Perpignan City Centre
Open: Monday to Saturday 11am to 7 pm.

**Directions:**

**Air:** Perpignan has a small airport just to the north of the town. Air France fly there from London via a Paris connection. Consequently, journey times can be up to six hours. Ryanair also fly to Perpignan, but only from a limited number of UK airports.
Buses from the airport stop at the Gare Routiere bus stop in the centre of town and at the SNCF railway station. It should take about 15 minutes.
Perpignan Airport: (33) 4 68526070
www.aeroport@perpignan.cci.fr
Because of the limited air services into Perpignan availability and higher prices can make a weekend jaunt quite expensive. One alternative is to fly to Toulouse-Blagnac and take the train journey south.

**Rail:** Take the TGV to Toulouse and change to the regional service. From Toulouse to Perpignan, there is one change at Narbonne, about an hour away. It is then a further hour by train to Perpignan.

**Tourist office:** For the tourist office, first head for Boulevard Wilson, west of Place de la Resistance, and then for the park and the giant exhibition centre called Palais des Congres.
Perpignan Office du Tourisme, Palais des Congres (00 33) 4 68663030
contact-office@little-france.com
www.perpignantourisme.com

**Accommodation:** Top end – La Villa Duflot, a four-star hotel. Prices for a twin or double start at around £100. Tel (00 33) 4 68565405
Sports fans on a flying visit are probably better off near the old town in the centre of Perpignan and the night scene. Expect to pay around the £60 mark for a double-room at the 3-star Hotel de France. There are various central 2-star hotels which seem good value at from £25 to £30 for a twin, but be prepared for some tired looking rooms. There are a limited number of chain hotels including the 100 IBIS (00 33) 4 68356262.

**Going out:** Perpignan, with its palm trees and public spaces, lives up to its Mediterranean setting. The brasseries and tapas restaurants of the Old Town are always busy. Try Quai Vauban on the canal's north bank, the venues around Place Arago. O' Shannon, an Irish pub, is on Rue de L'incendie, and Le Zinc, a cocktail bar, on Rue Grande des Fabriques. A former rugby player has set up a bar on the Quai Vauban; Imbeznon is popular with rugby fans.

# 3. Big match venues

These venues are listed by city, then stadium. Please note that for rugby league matches at these venues, tickets are often distributed by the RFL rather than the venue.

# Avignon

## Parc des Sports

**Ground:** Parc des Sports (Avignon)
**Address:** 13 Avenue Pierre De Coubertin, 8400 Avignon, France
**Phone** 33 4 90 88 29 10
**Capacity:** 17,518 (all seated)

**The stadium:** Parc des Sports is a multi-purpose stadium. The Ligue 2 football club AC Arles-Avignon play there. It was modernised in 2009, and has four stands. In 2011, 16,866 fans watched France play England in a rugby league international.

**Directions:**
**Air:** Avignon-Caumont airport (www.avignon.aeroport.fr) is 8km south-east of the town, but the nearest large airport for UK visitors is Marseille. Marseille to Avignon by road takes about an hour, traffic permitting. There is no train station at Marseille Airport, but there is a shuttle bus to Marseille (St Charles) station. If taking the train, the station in the centre of Avignon, instead of the TGV station outside of the city, can be a better choice. The latter offers a bus service into the city, but the local service offers a more convenient central location. To hire a car in Avignon take the train to the TGV station where the car rental companies are. Many trains from Marseilles to Avignon are local (TER), with no seat reservations. The TGV trains require advance bookings. The time varies between 36 and 90 minutes upwards. There are no direct buses from Marseille to Avignon. The bus trip is possible, with a change, probably in Aix-en-Provence.

**Rail:** Both Avignon's Gare SNCF and the adjacent Gare Routiere are just outside the walls south of the old city. The TGV station, 2km south, is linked by shuttle buses to Cours President -Kennedy.

**Road:** Driving into Avignon is a nightmare of junctions and one-way roads. The easiest parking is in two free, guarded car parks, linked to the centre by free shuttle buses: Ile Piot on the Ile de la Barthelasse and the riverside Parking des Italiens north east of town. Otherwise, the very busy parking garages inside the walls are expensive; check whether hotels offer parking.

**Accommodation:** Finding rooms in Avignon is often a problem: cheap hotels fill up, book in advance. Villeneuve-les-Avignon, across the river, may have rooms when Avignon is full. The tourist office can advise on hotels with vacancies. It is in the southern end of the city: 41 Cours Jean Jaures 04 32 74 32 74 www.avignon-tourisme.com

**Refreshments:** Avignon has an enormous number of restaurants, ranging from the expensively gastronomic to cheap snack places and takeaways.

# Bristol

## Memorial Stadium

**Address:** Filton Avenue, Horfield, Bristol BS7 0BF
**Phone:** 0117 909 6648
**Fax:** 0117 907 4312
**Website (Bristol Rovers FC):** www.bristolrovers.co.uk
**E-mail:**
**Capacity:** 11,858. Seated: 2,370. Standing: 9,478.

**The stadium:** Bristol Rovers moved to the stadium in 1996, and two years later bought the ground from Bristol Rugby Club. Although the Memorial Stadium has seen some changes since the football club took up residence, it still has the feel of a rugby club about it, which is perhaps not surprising because the ground is still shared with Bristol Rugby Club.
On one side is the DAS Stand, which with its pavilion looks more like a cricket stand. It has a row of hospitality boxes across the top, with a few rows of seats in front. Below is an area of terrace. The stand runs for about half the length of the pitch and straddles the halfway line. On one side of it, towards the Blackthorn end, is a small covered terrace, while the other side has a small covered area of temporary seating, called the South West Stand.
Opposite is the Uplands Stand, taller than the DAS Stand, but similar in length. This stand has covered seating to its rear and terracing at the front. It has open terracing to either side.
The team dug outs are located in front of the stand, although the dressing rooms are located behind the DAS Stand. This leads to a procession of players and officials at half and full-time.
At one end is the unusual looking South Stand. This was originally a temporary structure to fill this space. It has now been open for a number of seasons, although, with its green seats and bright white roof, looks for suitable for a show jumping competition. The stand only runs for just over half the width of the pitch and has several supporting pillars across the front. The other end, the Blackthorn End, is a covered terrace.

**Supporters with disabilities:** (As for Bristol Rovers FC matches) Over 30 accessible parking spaces, 20 to 50 yards from entrances. 13 spaces for wheelchair users at pitch side or concourse level. Three spaces for wheelchair users on raised platforms. No specific seating for ambulant disabled people. There are accessible toilets. Serving areas do not have low-level counters. There is no hearing loop installed. Radio commentary is available via radio links, but fans must bring their own headsets.

**Refreshments:** The Queen Vic pub on Gloucester Road is five minutes walk from the ground. It's not that big and does get busy.

The Annexe Inn, in Nevil Road, is about 10 minutes walk from the ground. Follow the signs for the County Cricket Ground.

**Directions:**

**Rail:** The nearest railway station is Filton Abbey Wood; 1.5 miles, a 20 to 25 minute walk to the ground.
Bristol Parkway is about two miles from the ground. Take a taxi or buses 73, 73A and 73B from the station to the stadium.

**Road:**
**From the North, West and East:** Exit the M4 at Junction 19 and join the M32. Go along the M32 for 3.1 miles and exit at Junction 2. Take the third exit signposted Horfield and Southmead. Follow the signs for Memorial Stadium.
Then join Muller Road and drive along it for 1.4 miles until a signal-controlled crossroads. Signposted right is Horfield Health Centre and Library. Ignore the sign and turn left into Filton Avenue. The ground is almost immediately on the left.

**From the South:**
Exit M5 at Junction 16 (signposted Filton) and join the A38 (south) towards Bristol City centre. The ground is about five miles down the A38. Pass the large British Aerospace works and further on, pass on the left the Inn on the Green and the Gloucester pubs. Then pass the Wellington pub on the right and continue along the A38, Gloucester Road, turn left into Filton Avenue. The entrance to the club car park is the second right down this road.

**Parking:** Parking is very difficult on Filton Avenue. The ground is in a busy residential area. Usually, finding a space within a five to 10 minute walk is relatively easy. Muller Road and Gloucester Road are popular. If they are full, there are other roads on the other side of Gloucester Road. Go past the Wellington pub along Kellaway Avenue and there is another area of roads suitable for matchday parking.

# Cardiff

## Millennium Stadium

**Stadium:** Millennium Stadium, Westgate Street, Cardiff CF10 1NS.
**Telephone:** 0870 013 8600
**Fax:** 029 2082 2474
**Website:** www.millenniumstadium.com
**E-mail:** info@millenniumstadium.com
**Capacity:** 74,500 (all seated)

**Introduction:** Cardiff is an easy city to get to with more and more flights coming through Cardiff International Airport, which has direct links to Europe and Ireland as well as many British cities. The city is also good rail and road links and in the city, transport is easy.
Compared to London and Paris, Cardiff is little more than a village (relative size). However, with the Millennium Stadium being in the middle of the city, only a few yards from the busiest shopping streets, it can get very busy on match days. It is usually a good idea to arrive early before the crowds, and leave after the inevitable congestion has died down.

**The stadium:** The Victorian engineer Isambard Kingdom Brunel diverted Cardiff's River Taff to enable him to bring the railway to the city. The drained area was used for sport, and was the location of the original Wales national rugby stadium. Named after a nearby hotel where players changed before matches, Cardiff Arms Park was the soul of Welsh rugby and plans to replace it horrified many fans. The Millennium Stadium took three years to build, and cost £150million. When it opened for Rugby Union World Cup 1999, it proved itself a worthy successor and is now the home of both the rugby and football national sides, with rock concerts and the British Speedway Grand Prix staged out of season. Rugby league World Cup matches were played there in 2000, and the Challenge Cup Final and Magic Weekend have also been staged at the stadium.
The stadium's soaring ship-like structure can be seen from all over the city, and on match days the atmosphere is unbeatable.
Cardiff's Millennium Stadium probably ranks as one of the perfect places in the world to watch a game of rugby. The Welsh have some of the most passionate rugby fans ever to grace a stand and they create an uplifting atmosphere throughout the impressively designed stadium. There are many bars and restaurants within the concrete dome and with its retractable roof, a wet afternoon will not mar the fans' enjoyment.
It is unlikely that you will have much say in where you sit but try to avoid the front three rows because your eyes will be level with the players' feet. Also, if you are in the very back row take a scarf. There is often a draught that whistles through the gaps of the stand.

**Other information:** There are bricks bearing the names of all the 1999 World Cup squads outside the gates by the river. There are a few spelt incorrectly. Look out particularly for a famous New Zealand fly-half. The stadium masts are the highest points of the Cardiff skyline at 93 metres. The electricity bill for three months for the stadium is £22,000.

**Supporters with disabilities:** The stadium has excellent facilities for the disabled and carers are allowed in free. Call 08442 777 888 for tickets. Some wheelchair views from the stands are not the best because people's backs can prevent a clear view. Commentary for the visually impaired is available from each merchandise and programme outlet. Contact: Jan Hill 02920 822427 access@wru.co.uk

**Refreshments:** There are 17 public bars, many of which have special machines capable of serving 12 pints in 20 seconds. They are needed to cater for a demand that will see a full ground drink more than a pub in a year. There are 16 food outlets in the stadium.

**Directions:**

**Air:** Cardiff International Airport. Located 10 miles south-west of the city centre. There is a rail link with Cardiff Central Station, as well as regular bus services into the city. Trains are the best option on match days, when traffic is heavy. 01446 711777 www.cwfly.com

**Rail:** Getting to Cardiff by train is the most popular option for any major event, so the trains are packed. This includes local trains if staying in a nearby town. Booking well ahead is recommended.
Cardiff has two train stations: Cardiff Central and Cardiff Queen Street. Both are only a five minute walk from the Millennium Stadium. Cardiff Central is the bigger and busier of the two stations. There are frequent links to London Paddington, West Wales and the North. Queen Street provides local and Valleys services. On match days Cardiff Central station is extremely busy, and crowd control measures are in place, both before and after the game. Seat reservations for all trains leaving Cardiff Central are suspended after a major event, and seats are on a first come, first served basis.
Ensure a seat on a train by walking 20 minutes to Queens Street Station and get a train to Cardiff Central. You are then already in the station while thousands wait outside.
The stadium is visible from Cardiff Central station.
First Great Western: 08457 000125
Virgin: 08457 222333
Wales and Borders: 0870 9000773
Valley Line local services: 02920 231978

**Road:** Directions are clearly given from the M4, with different access routes depending on match tickets. Be aware that the city centre will be restricted

to traffic on match day. The roads around the stadium are closed to vehicles at least two hours prior and after kick-off.
Usually Westgate Street and St Mary's Street are closed as well as the roads around the Civic Centre.

The M4 motorway skirts the city's northern suburbs and is less than an hour away from Bristol and Bath. Cardiff runs an efficient park-and-ride scheme. Depending on whether tickets are for the north or south of the Millennium Stadium, supporters are advised to use different junctions. Leave home early and avoid the worst of the congestion, but the return journey is a different matter.

**M4/Severn Bridge Tolls:** Users only pay to get into Wales. Tollbooths (automatic and manned) are situated on the Wales side of the bridge.

**Parking:** The advice is not to enter Cardiff by car close to an event, instead use the excellent park and ride services. Signs for the scheme begin on the motorways approaching the city. Opposing fans are sent to different parks all over the city. The system has won praise from fans for its efficiency. There are many large multi-storey and surface car-parks in the city. A voucher system operates in Cardiff's streets, usually costing about £1 an hour for a maximum of two hours. Vouchers are on sale in newsagents' shops around the city. Streets immediately around the stadium are closed for up to two hours before and after matches.

**Bus:** Cardiff's Central Bus Station is a short walk from the ground.
There are direct coach links from major cities across the UK.
www.cardiffbus.com

**Coach:** National Express 08705 808080

**Stadium tours:** Sports fan or not, a tour behind the scenes at the Millennium Stadium is a must. Visit the dressing rooms and walk on the pitch, the royal box and take in the view from the top of the stands.
029 2082 2228. 10am to 5pm Monday to Saturday. 10am to 4pm Sundays and Bank Holidays. No tours on event and match days
Booking essential, pay on arrival (Gate 3): £3.50 (2013).

**Refreshments outside the stadium:** Pubs fill up early on match days, but drinking on the streets outside the pubs is common. St Mary's Street has the Oz Bar and The Walkabout able to accommodate large groups of fans. Berlins Venue Bar in Church Street also has a giant screen and multiple television screens around each of its three bars.

**Merchandise:** The merchandise shop sits behind the stadium opposite the coach station, mainly rugby union items.

**Tourist Office:** The Old Library, The Hayes, Cardiff CF10 1AH.
029 2087 3573. www.visitcardiff.com

# Limerick

# Thomond Park

**Stadium:** Thomond Park
**Stadium address:** Thomond Park, Cratloe Road, Limerick
**Telephone:** 061 42 1100
**Fax:** 061 42 1135
**Website:** thomondpark.i.e.
**E-mail:** info@thomondpark.ie
**Capacity:** 25,630. **Seating:** 15,100; **standing:** 10,530.

**The Stadium:** Thomond Park and Munster Rugby have a special place in rugby union history. Since the professional era began Munster's record in Thomond Park has been fantastic, both in the domestic league and European (Heineken Cup) competitions.
In 1998 and 1999 following the introduction of the professional era, the Irish Rugby Football Union (who own the ground) invested in floodlighting, terracing, toilets, medical facilities and a new pitch.
In March 2006 the IRFU and Munster Rugby announced that Thomond Park was selected for the site of a new stadium. Work started in early 2007, and the project was completed for a reopening in the autumn of 2008. Two new stands were built, making the capacity 25,630. The stadium hosted its first rugby league game when Ireland took on France on 5 November 2011.

**Directions:**

**Air:** There are many direct flights from the UK to Shannon International Airport. If flights are fully booked, Cork Airport, 60 miles from Limerick, is a good bet with most major airlines making the connection with the UK.

**Sea and road:** Ferry from Swansea to Cork (crossing takes 10 hours)
Limerick is about two hours drive from Cork.
Ferry from Pembroke to Rosslare (crossing takes 3.5 hours)
Limerick is about four hours drive from Rosslare.
Ferry from Holyhead to Dublin (crossing 1.75 to 3.5 hours), then three hour drive to Limerick

**From Limerick City Centre:** Turn left at the junction between O'Connell and William Street and go on the Sarsfields Bridge. Continue for about 400 yards to the Ennis-Shelbourne Road Junction. Turn right at the traffic lights and go straight onto the next set of lights, turn left and Thomond Park is opposite.

**Parking:** Normally public parking is not permitted in the vicinity of the stadium on match days, and some local roads are closed. There are park and ride services from various venues in the city.

**Rail:** The closest station to Thomond Park is Colbert Station, Parnell Street, Limerick. There are direct inter-city services from Dublin and Cork. It's a long walk to Thomond Park from Colbert Station, and it's advisable to get a taxi.

**By foot:** The stadium is in the north west corner of town, a 30 to 40 minute walk from the city centre. There are plenty of pubs that line the way. There are two routes to the ground. One option is to take Thomond Bridge by King John's Castle and walk for just under a mile towards Hasset's Cross junction, look out for the floodlights.
Alternatively, cross Sarsfield Bridge and walk for about half a mile before turning into Shelbourne Road at Union Cross. At Hasset's Cross, at the next set of lights go left.

**In the city:** The city centre is south of the river and revolves around O'Connell Street. The tourist office is the centre on Arthurs Quay. The bus and train station is to the south of O'Connell Street.

**Stadium tour:** The one hour full stadium tour consists of a museum visit and film, entry to the home and away dressing rooms, plus visits to pitch-side and the Munster dugout.

**Supporters with disabilities:** There are facilities and entrances in the West Stand, and designated parking nearby.

**Local refreshments:** Limerick is a university city with a student population of around 20,000. It has also been described as a city with a town atmosphere. Don't expect too many bright lights. However, as well as the history and the culture there are clubs, bars and restaurants in Limerick. Many former Munster players have set up bars or hotels in the city. So there are plenty of venues that understand and cater for a rugby crowd. One such watering hole is *The Claw* at Howley's Quay, owned by Peter Clohessy, a former Ireland and Munster prop. Fans could also head for Dolan's Bar and Restaurant on Dock Road. The Brazen Head Sports Bar at 103 O'Connell Street has big screens and sporting memorabilia while for something more old-fashioned, try The Locke Bar at 3 George's Quay, one of Limerick's oldest pubs.

# London

**Using public transport in London:** The Oyster Card system covers buses, underground and trains in the Greater London area, except for the Heathrow Express. It is considerably cheaper to use an Oyster card than buying paper tickets. Visitors can buy a pay as you go Oyster card at most stations, and put money on it for their trip. It can then be used on future visits to London.

# Richmond Athletic Ground

**Stadium address:** The Athletic Ground, Kew Foot Road, Richmond, Surrey TW9 2SS
**Telephone:** 020 8940 7156
**Fax:** 020 8940 0342
**Capacity:** 4,000. Seated: 851

**The stadium:** The Richmond Athletic Ground in south-west London, normally home to the Championship Rugby Union side London Scottish and Richmond RFC. It was the venue for the annual Oxford versus Cambridge Varsity rugby league match from 1997 to 2005, and again in 2012.
There is one stand, capable of seating around 1,000 people, though in the past temporary stands have been erected in the considerable space around the pitch to boost seating capacity. Part of a large leisure complex, the rugby part is bordered by a swimming pool, a golf club, a bowls club and a health centre.

**Refreshments:** There is a bar at the ground. There are also plenty of places to eat in Richmond town centre and at the station.

**Directions:**

**Richmond station has both train and underground services.**
**Rail:** South West trains from Waterloo or Clapham Junction. London Overground from Stratford.
**Underground:** District Line.
Turn right out of the station and cross the A316 at the traffic lights.
Turn left and the ground is 50 yards on the right.

**Road:** The ground is on the A316, between Richmond roundabout and Richmond Baths.
Turn right on slip road if heading out of town, and left if heading in. It has good transport links to the South Circular Road (A205) and the M3, which links directly to the A316 after its junction with the M25.

**Parking:** The ground has considerable parking facilities for its size. There is also a public car park across the A316. Local streets often are residents only and are busy.

## The Honourable Artillery Company

**Stadium address:** The Honourable Artillery Company, Armoury House, City Road, London EC1Y 2BQ
**Telephone:** 020 7382 1533 (Events sales office. Wedding can be held here if you can afford it)
**Website:** http://the.hac.org.uk
**Capacity:** Around 1,000

The Honourable Artillery Company was incorporated by Royal Charter in 1537 by Henry VIII. The current HAC Regiment forms part of the Territorial Army and is part of the 1st Artillery Brigade. Members of the Regiment are drawn for the most part from young professional men and women working in and around the City. It hosts the regular pre-season friendly between London Broncos and London Skolars, and hosted the 2013 Oxford versus Cambridge Varsity rugby league match.

**The stadium:** The rugby field is on one side of a cricket pitch. There is no spectator accommodation, though a temporary stand has been erected occasionally.

**Refreshments:** A bar is available on match days, and there are plenty of local cafes, snack bars etc, although they can be busy at lunchtime. A pre-match hospitality lunch is often available for the rugby league matches staged here, but must be pre-booked.

**Directions:**

**Rail:** Closest train stations:
Liverpool Street (approximately a 10 minute walk); Moorgate (approximately a five minute walk)

**Underground:** Moorgate: (walk north on City Road); Old Street (Exit 5 walk south down City Road)
Both underground stations are a five minute walk to the HAC.

**Road:** The ground is in the London Congestion Zone. Go south on City Road from the Old Street roundabout, which is on the inner London ring road (A501).

**Parking:** If it is necessary to drive there is an NCP car park at Finsbury Square almost opposite the HAC. There is no parking at the HAC other than for pre-booked disabled badge holders. The property frontage on City Road has a 'castle' appearance and is situated directly next to 32–36 City Road and opposite the Travelodge.

## Wembley Stadium

**Address:** Empire Way, Wembley, London HA9 0WS
**Postal address:** Wembley Stadium, PO Box 1966, London SW1P 9EQ
**Main phone number:** 0844 980 8001
**Website:** www.wembleystadium.com
**Capacity:** 90,000 (all seated)

**The stadium:** The stadium is totally enclosed and comprises three tiers, with both sides of the stadium being slightly larger than the ends. Both these side stands have large upper and lower tiers, with a smaller middle tier sandwiched in between. The stadium has a roof which appears retractable, but only one third can be moved. The most striking external feature is The Arch, towering some 133 metres above the stadium. It comprises of white tubular steel and can be seen for many miles across London.
In front of the stadium is a bronze statue of Bobby Moore. It gazes down on fans approaching the stadium along Wembley Way, and a useful place to meet friends pre-match. There are also plans to build a statue of rugby league players.
Although not the most generous of leg room, it is still more than adequate and there is a good height between rows. The top tier (Level 5) is particularly steep, which may put a few people out of breath.
Nonetheless, the main problem with Wembley is the same now as when the Empire Stadium opened in 1923, it's in Wembley. Wembley may be close to a network of railways and motorways but it can still be a pain to get to.

**Links to rugby league:** The Rugby League Challenge Cup Final has been played annually at the old Wembley Stadium since 1929, when Wigan were the victors. The Cup Final returned to its traditional home in 2007 after the re-building of Wembley. International rugby returned to Wembley in 2007 when Wales lost to New Zealand and Australia beat England in the Rugby League Four Nations.

**Supporters with disabilities:**
E-mail: accessforall@wembleystadium.com
Website: www.wembleystadium.com/brilliantfuture/accessforAll
For information on parking phone CS parking on 0208 795 1758
There are 310 accessible wheelchair user spaces and associated carer/PA seats available across all levels of the stadium. All information desks and kiosks, bars and points of sale have induction loop facilities. There are 147 accessible toilets within the stadium, with access controlled by use of a Radar key. There are 100 enhanced amenity seats for ambulant disabled visitors and those accompanied by assistance dogs.

**Refreshments:** Apparently there is one refreshment till per 100 spectators inside the stadium and this seems to work well with reasonable queues. Food and drink prices are on the high side. The concourses themselves are mostly fairly spacious, have betting as well as food outlets, and numerous flat-screened televisions.
Bottles and cans cannot be brought into the stadium.

**Directions**

**Air:** From Heathrow Airport: The most direct route is by Heathrow Express to Paddington, with one change onto the westbound Bakerloo line travelling direct to Wembley Central. This takes about 60 minutes and costs £23. A cheaper option is to use the Piccadilly Line, and change at Green Park onto the Jubilee line.

From Gatwick Airport: Take the Gatwick Express to Victoria station. Then take the Victoria Line to Green Park and change to the Jubilee line to Wembley Park. This will take about 90 minutes.

From Stansted Airport: Take the Stansted Express to Liverpool Street main line station, change to the westbound Metropolitan Line and travel direct to Wembley Park. This takes around 90 minutes and costs £26

**Train and underground:** The nearest underground station is Wembley Park which is around a 15 minute walk from the stadium. This is served by both the Jubilee and Metropolitan lines, although it is best to take the latter as it has fewer stops.
Wembley Central is slightly further away from the stadium and has both train and underground connections. The underground station is served by the Bakerloo line, while the railway station is on the London Euston-Milton Keynes line.
The nearest train station is Wembley Stadium which is on the London Marylebone to Birmingham line. This is a good way of getting to the stadium from central London, the journey from Marylebone is about 10 minutes.

**Bus:** London bus routes : 83 Golders Green to Ealing Hospital; 92 St Raphael's North to Ealing Hospital; 182 Brent Cross to Harrow Weald; 206 Kilburn Park to Wembley Park; 223 Wembley to Harrow; 224 Wembley Stadium Station to St Raphael's Estate; 297 Willesden to Ealing Broadway.

**Road:** The stadium has been designated as a 'public transport' destination, meaning that there is very limited parking available at the stadium itself, and what there is is expensive. There is also a residents only parking scheme in operation in the local area. Unless fans have booked in advance, it is not recommended to drive to the stadium.
The stadium is well signposted from the end of the M1 and M40, and from the A406 North Circular Road.

One suggestion is to park at a tube station on the Metropolitan line such as Uxbridge, Hillingdon or Ruislip, or at Stanmore on the Jubilee line, and then take the tube to Wembley Park
The roads around Wembley get clogged post-match, and though there are queues for the tube, queues are well-managed and it shouldn't be too long before you are on a train.
Realistically, unless you are a VIP, or on a coach, don't drive to Wembley.

**Stadium tours:** There are daily tours of the stadium. These last about 75minutes and cost £16 for adults and £9 concessions. There is a VIP tour for £45. To Book: Phone: 0844 800 2755.
www.wembleystadium.com/wembley-tours

**Local refreshments:** There are not many pubs close to the stadium. The few pubs that are close by such as J.J. Moons (Wetherspoons), the Green Man (both near Wembley Stadium station) and the Torch (near Wembley Park tube station) are usually heaving many hours before kick-off.
An additional problem is that they may designate themselves as only allowing entrance to one team's fans.
Most fans tend to either drink in the centre of London before a game, or near one of the tube stations north of the stadium.
There is a Subway opposite Wembley Park station, and local shops, and various cafes and take aways near Wembley Central.

## Big match venues

Old Trafford welcomes the Grand Final.

The Honourable Artillery Ground in the City of London.

# Manchester

## Etihad Stadium

**Address:** Sportcity, Rowsley Street, Manchester M11 3FF
**Main phone Number:** 0161 444 1894
**Main fax number:** 0151 438 7999
**Website (Manchester City FC):** www.mcfc.co.uk
**Capacity:** 48,000 (all seated)

**Stadium history:** The stadium was originally built for the 2002 Commonwealth Games at a cost of £90m. Post-games, Manchester City FC moved in as permanent tenants, and spent another £20m refitting it. The running track was removed and the stands extended. A roof was added to one end. The stadium was named the City of Manchester stadium by Manchester City Council before construction began in December 1999. There are some commonly used alternatives; Eastlands refers to the site and the stadium before they were named SportCity. The stadium was renamed the Etihad Stadium by the club in July 2011 as part of 10 year agreement with the team kit sponsors Etihad Airways.

**The stadium:** After playing at Maine Road for 80 years, Manchester City FC moved to the City of Manchester Stadium in August 2003. The stadium has a bowl design and is totally enclosed, with three tiers of seating at the sides, and two tiers at each end. While the seating is continuous, each side of the stadium is named in the manner of a traditional football ground. Initially, all sides were named by compass direction (North Stand and South Stand for the ends, East Stand and west Stand for the sides) but in February 2004, after a vote by fans, the West Stand was renamed the Colin Bell Stand in honour of the former Manchester City player. The club have plans to redevelop the area around the stadium, which would include an increase in capacity to 60,000 by adding an additional tier to both ends.

**Links to rugby league:** In October 2004 the stadium played host to an international between Great Britain and Australia in the Tri-Nations series in front of nearly 40,000 spectators. The stadium hosted the Magic Weekend on 26 and 27 May 2012. In the 1940s and 1950s, the Championship Final was often played at Maine Road, the football clubs' former home.

**Refreshments:** The facilities are good with spacious concourses, large television screens showing the game and a good selection of food. There is a large area just outside the stadium, where supporters can drink and eat in a covered area before and after matches. There are two large bars, one for food and one for drinks.

**Local refreshments:** There are not many pubs near the stadium. The Stanley is about 10 minutes walk from the stadium, just back from the main

A6010 (Pottery Lane), towards Ashburys station. Also the Townley on Albert Street is a five minute walk from the stadium. In the city centre, The Printworks, near Victoria Station, has pubs, and food outlets.

**Supporters with disabilities:** There are 182 spaces for wheelchair users, an induction loop system, 30 accessible toilets, and facilities for ambulant disabled supporters to sit with their assistants / carers as required. Parking facilities for supporters with disabilities are in the stadium complex. Assistance dogs welcome, but must be booked in advance. More information on the Manchester City website in the 'Access' section.

**Directions:**

**Train:** The stadium is located to the east of Manchester city centre. Ashburys is the nearest railway station, a 20 minute walk from the stadium, services are limited. Turn left out of the station and after proceeding up the road you will come to the stadium on the left. Manchester Piccadilly, which has mainline trains is a 30 minute walk along a signposted route. The Etihad Campus Metrolink station on the Manchester Metrolink is close to Joe Mercer Way. The trip from Piccadilly is about 10 minutes.

**Taxi:** A taxi from Piccadilly Station is about £6.

**Bus:** From Piccadilly Gardens: go down the main approach from the station, then along London Road to Piccadilly Gardens; normal service and special matchday buses leave from the right hand side of the square, £1 each way. To return, the special buses leave from Ashton New Road.

**Road:** The stadium is located in the north east of Manchester.

**From the South, M6:** Leave the M6 at Junction 19. Follow the A556 towards Stockport and then join the M56 going towards Stockport. Continue onto the M60, passing Stockport and heading on towards Ashton-under-Lyne. Leave the M60 at Junction 23 and take the A635 towards Manchester. Branch onto A662 (Ashton New Road) towards Droylesden and Manchester. Stay on A662 for around three miles and stadium is on the right.

**From M62:** Leave M62 at junction 18. Join M60 (south and west) towards Ashton-under-Lyne. Leave M60 at junction 23, take A635 towards Manchester. Branch onto A662 (Ashton New Road) towards Droylesden and Manchester. Stay on A662 for three miles and stadium is on the right.

**Parking:** Some parking available at the stadium, about £10 per car. A residents only parking scheme covers streets about a mile out from the stadium. Some unofficial car parks charge around £5 a car. The road links are busy even on non-match days, allow plenty of time.

**Stadium tours:** Manchester City FC offer daily tours of the stadium, cost £8.50 for adults, and £6 for concessions. Tours should be booked in advance, phone 0161 444 1894.

# Old Trafford

**Address:** Sir Matt Busby Way, Manchester M16 0RA
**Main Phone Number:** 0161 868 8000
**Main Fax number** 0161 868 8804
**Capacity:** 76,100 (All-Seated)

**The stadium:** Old Trafford is billed as 'The Theatre of Dreams'. It has always been a special place, and its sheer size makes it a bewildering sight. Both ends, which look almost identical, are large two-tiered stands. Each is steep, with a large lower tier and smaller upper tier.
The three-tiered Sir Alex Ferguson Stand at one side of the ground has the largest capacity of any club ground in England. The corners each side of the North Stand are also filled with seating and extend around to meet both ends. These redeveloped stands dwarf the older (South) Stand on the opposite side. This stand is single-tiered, with a television gantry suspended below its roof.
Unusual aspects of the ground include the raised pitch, and that the teams enter the field from the corner of the Main Stand. Outside the ground look out for is the Sir Matt Busby Statue fronting the impressive green-glassed East Stand façade. There is also a clock and plaque in remembrance of the Munich disaster.

**Links to rugby league:** Old Trafford has regularly played host to rugby league. The first game of Rugby League at the Theatre of Dreams was a Lancashire fixture against the New Zealand tourists in 1924-5. There was then a bit of a gap, until a one-off league match between Salford and Leeds in 1958. Links between Manchester United and the code go back further than that however, because the club had taken over the old Broughton Rangers ground at The Cliff, for training, reserve and youth games
The first rugby league test match played at Old Trafford came in 1986, when Australia beat Great Britain 28–16 with 50,583 present.
The following year Old Trafford hosted the Premiership final for the first time, when Wigan defeated Warrington 8–0. The Super League Grand Final has been played here since the introduction of the play-off system in 1998. Old Trafford was chosen as the venue for the 2000 World Cup Final; 44,329 saw Australia defeat New Zealand 40–12. And, of course, it is already booked for the 2013 World Cup Final.

### How to get to the city

**Air:** Manchester Airport is located eight miles away from Old Trafford. Either get a taxi from the airport (around £20), or catch one of the regular train services (seven per hour) from the airport to Manchester Piccadilly Station (journey time 15-25 mins depending on service caught).
Change there for another train or Metrolink tram to Old Trafford.

**Train:** Probably the best way to get to the stadium is by Metrolink (tram) or train from Manchester Piccadilly station, as Old Trafford has both its own railway station next to the ground, and a Metrolink station which is located next to Lancashire County Cricket Club on Warwick Road, which leads up to Sir Matt Busby Way. Normally the railway station is less busy than the Metrolink. Or get a bus from Piccadilly Gardens (see below).
The Metrolink also has another branch line going to Eccles from Manchester Centre. There are two stops to leave the train-Pomona and Exchange Quay. There are on the opposite (Salford) side of the ground-probably a quieter line on matchdays. Pomona is the closest to the ground, only a short walk away and closer than Lancashire CC. Exchange Quay is the one to use for return journeys as the trams get full and may not stop at Pomona going back.
However, if you have a train to catch after the game, avoid Old Trafford Metrolink at all costs. The best bet is to get the train from Manchester United Football Ground station to Piccadilly. (Journey time 10 mins)

**Bus:** Manchester Coach Station is located three miles away from Old Trafford. However, it is only a few minutes walk away from Piccadilly Train station, where a train or metro can be caught to the ground, or Piccadilly Gardens, where local buses can be found.
Come out of the main coach station entrance turn right along Chorlton Street. At the bottom of Chorlton Street, turn left into Aytoun Street. Proceed along this road and then turn right into Auburn Street. At the crossroads with London Road, the entrance to the station is on the right. Continue past the station and at the next junction turn left, into Piccadilly Gardens where there is a large bus terminus.
From Piccadilly Gardens get the Stagecoach Manchester Busses 255, 256 or Arriva North West No. 263. These services all run down the A56 Chester Road near to Old Trafford. Journey time, depending as always on traffic, is around 15 to 20 minutes.

**Road:**

**From the South:** Leave the M6 at Junction 19 and follow the A556 towards Altrincham. This leads onto the A56 towards Manchester. Keep on the A56 for six miles and then come to Sir Matt Busby Way on the left.
The ground is half a mile down this road on the left, although on matchdays the road will be closed to traffic.
From other destinations: M60 junction 7 and M56, or M602 off M60.

**Parking:** There are lots of small private car parks near to the ground, otherwise it is street parking, which is limited.
Try Old Trafford Cricket Ground (£10), but arrive as early as possible , as it takes ages to get out after the game. Alternatively, the Salford Quays Lowry

Mall is a ten minute walk from the stadium, and costs about £3.50. The road goes onto the M602 which joins up with the M62/M6.
There is also the MediaCityUK multi-storey car park located at Salford Quays. It has 2,300 places and is only a 10 minute walk from Old Trafford. The car park is easily accessible via junction 2 on the M602. For a three-hour stay the cost will be about £4.50. Another option is to park near one of the tram stops south of the stadium, and get the tram to Old Trafford.

Media CityUK is worth a visit. The piazza is a wonderful outdoor space located in front of the studios, with a newly-installed double-sided outdoor screen. There is the Lowry Arts Centre and the Imperial War Museum MediaCityUK also hosts a variety of restaurants.

**Stadium tours:** There are daily tours of Old Trafford (except on matchdays, which include the club museum, and cost £15 for adults, £10 concessions to book, call 0161 868 8000

**Supporters with disabilities:** Old Trafford has good facilities for supporters with disabilities, full details at www.mudsa.org
Contact at Old Trafford: Phil Downs 0845 230 1989 disability@manutd.com

Parking for wheelchair users is about 50 metres from the disabled supporters' entrance to the stadium in a dedicated car park. From the car park there is a considerable slope down to the entrance point with level access within the stadium.
There are up to 120 spaces for wheelchair users. Most are in a covered, three-tiered area in the South-East corner of the stadium. However, some are at the top of the new quadrants, accessed via lifts. Places for ambulant disabled supporters are located in the lower East stand.

Eight accessible toilets are located adjacent to the disabled supporters area, two of which are within the disabled supporters lounge (The Albany Suite) This is an interactive suite for disabled users only and has full refreshment facilities at a low-level counter. There are 20 seats available with match commentary, together with a further 20 places for PA's seated adjacent. Radio headsets are available on match-days.

**Refreshments:** The pubs nearest the ground are The Trafford, Sam Platts and The Bishops Blaze. These don't normally allow away (football) fans in. Or drink in the city centre or along one of the stops on the Metrolink, such as Altrincham or Sale. The Quadrant pub is about a 15 minute walk from Old Trafford, towards the cricket ground, and has a couple of takeaways nearby. There is also the Lime Bar in nearby Salford Quays

# Scotland

**Scotland rugby league website:** http://scotlandrl.com
**Address:** Scotland Rugby League, Caledonia House, 1 Redheughs Rigg, South Gyle, Edinburgh, EH12 9DQ

### Boroughmuir

**Stadium:** Meggetland, Colinton Road, Edinburgh EH14 1AS
**Website:** www.boroughmuirsports.co.uk
**Phone** 0131 443 7571
This stadium staged both Scotland's Alitalia European Cup matches in 2012

### Glasgow Hawks

**Stadium:** The Pavilion, Old Anniesland, 689 Crow Road, Glasgow GL13 1PL
**Website:** www.glasgowhawks.com
**Phone:** 0141 950 1222
**Fax:** 0141 950 1222

### Glasgow Warriors

**Stadium:** The Scotstoun Stadium, 72 Danes Drive, Glasgow G14 9HD
**Capacity:** 9,708
**Website:** www.glasgowwarriors.org
**E-mail:** info@glasgowwarriors.org
**Phone:** 0141 954 5100
**Fax:** 0141 959 9570
This stadium staged the Scotland versus Ireland match in 2011.

### Murrayfield

**Stadium:** Murrayfield Stadium, Edinburgh EH12 5PJ
**Website:** www.edinburghrugby.org
**E-mail:** info@edinburghrugby.org
**Phone:** 0131 346 5000
**Fax:** 0131 346 5001
**Capacity:** 67,130

In 2000 and 2002 the Rugby League Challenge Cup Final was held at Murrayfield. Both games were played in front of over 60,000 fans, easily the biggest gates for rugby league in Scotland. The Magic Weekend has also been held here.

# 4. National Conference League

Askam
Blackbrook
Bradford Dudley Hill
Castleford Panthers
Coventry Bears
Crosfields
Dewsbury Celtic
East Hull
East Leeds
Eastmoor Dragons
Eccles
Egremont Rangers
Elland
Featherstone Lions
Heworth
Hindley
Hull Dockers
Hunslet Warriors
Ince Rose Bridge
Kells
Leigh East
Leigh Miners Rangers
Lock Lane
Milford Marlins
Millom
Myton Warriors
Normanton Knights
Oldham St Annes
Oulton Raiders
Ovenden
Peterlee Pumas
Pilkington Recs
Rochdale Mayfield
Saddleworth Rangers
Shaw Cross Sharks
Siddal
Skirlaugh
Stanley Rangers
Stanningley
Thatto Heath Crusaders
Underbank Rangers
Waterhead
Wath Brow Hornets
West Hull
Widnes West Bank
Wigan St Cuthbert's
Wigan St Jude's
Wigan St Patrick's
Woolston Rovers
York Acorn

It is strongly recommended to check venue and kick off times before travelling to National Conference League matches.

**Askam**
**Ground:** Fallowfield Park, Sandy Lane, Askam in Furness LA16 7BD
**Website:** www.askamrl.com
**E-mail:**
**Phone:** 01229 463320
**Fax:** 01229 463320

**Blackbrook Royals**
**Ground:** Blackbrook Sports & Recreation Club, Boardmans Lane, St Helens WA11 9BB
**Website:** www.blackbrookarlfc.co.uk
**E-mail:** info@blackbrookarlfc.co.uk
**Phone:** 01744 730492

**Bradford Dudley Hill**
**Ground:** The Neil Hunt Memorial Ground, Lower Lane, Bradford BD4 8TJ
**Website:** www.pitchero.com/clubs/bradforddudleyhillarlfc
**E-mail:** dudley.hill@hotmail.co.uk
**Phone:** 01274 669276

**Castleford Panthers**
**Ground:** Three Lane Ends, Raglan Close, Castleford WF10 1PL
**Website:** www.pitchero.com/clubs/castlefordpanthersarlfc
**E-mail:** castleford_panthers@yahoo.co.uk
**Phone:** 01977 513309

**Coventry Bears**
**Ground:** Butts Park Arena, Coventry CV1 3GE
**Website:** www.coventrybears.co.uk
**E-mail:** alan.robinson@coventrybears.co.uk
**Phone:** 07974 517519
Also play at: Xcel Leisure Centre, Canley, Coventry CV4 8DY

**Crosfields**
**Ground:** Hood Lane Recreation Ground, Hood Lane North, Warrington Cheshire WA5 1ET
**Website:** www.pitchero.com/clubs/crosfieldsarlfc
**E-mail:** crosfieldsarlfc@yahoo.co.uk
**Phone:** 01925 411730

**Dewsbury Celtic**
**Ground:** Park Parade, Westtown, Dewsbury WF13 2QJ
**Website:** www.pitchero.com/clubs/dewsburycelticrlfc
**E-mail:** michrugby13@btinternet.com
**Phone:** 01924 462615

**East Hull**
**Ground:** Rosmead Sports Centre, Rosmead Street, Southcoates Lane Hull HU9 2TA
**Website:** www.pitchero.com/clubs/easthull
**E-mail:** ullswater1@ullswater1.karoo.co.uk
**Phone:** 01482 709529

**East Leeds**
**Ground:** Richmond Hill, 81 Easy Road, Leeds LS9 8QS
**Website:** www.pitchero.com/clubs/eastleedsarlfc
**Phone:** 0113 240 2503

**Eccles**
**Ground:** Moat Hall Sports Centre, Hallsworth Road, Eccles M30 7LS
**Website:** www.ecclesrugbyleague.co.uk
**E-mail:** info@ecclesrugbyleague.co.uk
**Phone:** 0161 788 0011
**Fax:** 0161 788 0011

**Egremont Rangers**
**Ground:** Gillfoot Park, North Road, Egremont CA22 2PR
**Website:** www.pitchero.com/clubs/egremontrangersarlfc
**E-mail:** crosswater1@tiscali.co.uk
**Phone:** 01946 820798

**Elland**
**Ground:** Greetland Community Centre, Rochdale Road, Greetland, Halifax HX4 8JG
**Website:** www.pitchero.com/clubs/ellandarlfc
**E-mail:** soozjordan@hotmail.co.uk
**Phone:** 01422 370140

**Featherstone Lions**
**Ground:** The Mill Pond Ground, Wakefield Road, Featherstone, Pontefract WF7 5DX
**Website:** www.featherstonelions.co.uk
**E-mail:** info@featherstonelions.co.uk
**Phone:** 01977 790278
**Fax:** 01977 707083

**Heworth**
**Ground:** Elmpark Way, Stockton Lane, Heworth, York YO31 1DX
**Website:** www.heworth-arlfc.co.uk
**E-mail:** hewortharlfc@hotmail.co.uk
**Phone:** 01904 421075
**Fax:** 01904 421 075

**Hull Dockers**
**Ground:** The Willows Sports and Social Club, 695A Holderness Road Hull HU8 9AN
**Website:** www.pitchero.com/clubs/hulldockers
**E-mail:** info@hulldockersrugby.co.uk
**Phone:** 01482 376404

**Hunslet Warriors**
**Ground:** The Oval, Hunslet, Leeds LS10 2AT
**Website:** www.hunsletwarriors.co.uk
**E-mail:** pamcrosby@btopenworld.com

**Ince Rose Bridge**
**Ground:** Pinfold Street, Manchester Road, Higher Ince, Wigan WN2 2DZ
**Website:** www.pttchero.com/clubs/incerosebridgeopenarfc
**E-mail:** incerosebridge@hotmail.com
**Phone:** 01942 244111

**Leigh East**
**Ground:** Leigh Sports Village, Ledgard Avenue, Leigh WN7 4GY
**Website:** www.leigheast.org.uk
**E-mail:** information@leigheast.org.uk
**Phone:** 01942 510 208

**Leigh Miners Rangers**
**Ground:** Leigh Miners Welfare Sports & Social Club, Twist Lane, Leigh WN7 4EF
**Website:** www.leighminersrangers.net
**E-mail:** info@leighrangersminers.net
**Phone:** 01942 672984
**Fax:** 01942 671782

**Lock Lane**
**Ground:** Lock Lane Sports Centre, Lock Lane, Castleford WF10 2JU
**Website:** www.pitchero.com/clubs/castlefordlocklanearlfc
**E-mail:** locklanesportscentre@hotmail.com
**Phone:** 01977 731 233
**Fax:** 01977 510 676

**Milford Marlins**
**Ground:** Milford Sports Club, Beecroft Street, Kirkstall, Leeds LS5 3AS
**Website:** www.pitchero.com/clubs/milfordmarlinsarlfc
**E-mail:** charles.bray1@ntlworld.com
**Phone:** 01132 263030

**Millom**
**Ground:** Coronation Field, Devonshire Road, Millom, Cumbria LA18 4PG
**Website:** www.millomrlfc.co.uk
**E-mail:** davewarren67@hotmail.co.uk
**Phone:** 01229 772030
**Fax:** 01229 770388

**Myton Warriors**
**Ground:** Marist Sporting Club, Cranbrook Avenue, Hull HU6 7TX
**Website:** www.mytonwarriorsarlc.co.uk
**E-mail:** desifox@hotmail.co.uk
**Phone:** 01482 859216

**Normanton Knights**
**Ground:** Queen Elizabeth Drive, Normanton WF6 1DT
**Website:** www.pitchero.com/clubs/normantonknightsarlfc
**E-mail:** k_daw@sky.com
**Phone:** 01924 897081

**Oldham St Anne's**
**Ground:** Higginshaw Road, Oldham OL1 3JY
**Website:** www.oldhamstannes.co.uk
**E-mail:** babs261046@yahoo.co.uk
**Phone:** 0161 678 8660

**Oulton Raiders**
**Ground:** Oulton Sports Pavilion, Oulton Green, Leeds LS26 8EL
**Website:** www.oultonraiders.com
**E-mail:** secretary@oultonraiders.com
**Phone:** 0113 282 2356

**Ovenden**
**Ground:** Four Fields, Cousin Lane, Halifax HX2 8AD
**Website:** www.pitchero.com/clubs/ovendenarlfc
**E-mail:**
**Phone:** 01422 347739

**Rochdale Mayfield**
**Ground:** Mayfield Sports Centre, Keswick Street, Castleton, Rochdale OL11 3BY. N.B If using sat nav do not exit the M62 at Heywood – the Club is not accessible from the Heywood end of Chadwick Lane.
**Website:** www.mayfieldrl.co.uk
**E-mail:** rochdalemayfieldsec@live.co.uk
**Phone:** 01706 527103

**Saddleworth Rangers**
**Ground:** Shaw Hill Bank Road, Greenfield, Oldham OL3 7LD
**Website:** www.pitchero.com/clubs/saddleworthrangersarlfc
**E-mail:** webmaster@saddleworthrangers.co.uk
**Phone:** 01457 876077

**Shaw Cross Sharks**
**Ground:** Leeds Road, Dewsbury WF12 7HP
**Website:** www.shawxsharks.com
**E-mail:**
**Phone:** 01924 463987

**Siddal**
**Ground:** Siddal Sports & Community Centre, Chevinedge, Exley Lane Halifax HX3 9EW
**Website:** www.siddalarlfc.co.uk
**E-mail:**
**Phone:** 01422 367376

**Skirlaugh Bulls**
**Ground:** Eastside Community Sports & Social Club, Slaithes Lane, Saltend Hedon, Hull HU12 8DS.
**Website:** www.pitchero.com/clubs/skirlaughbulls
**E-mail:** rlgilly@hotmail.com
**Phone:** 01482 896113

**Stanley Rangers**
**Ground:** Stanley Sports & Social Club, Lee Moor Road, Stanley, Wakefield WF3 4EQ
**Website:** www.stanleyrangers.org.uk
**E-mail:** stanleyrangers@hotmail.co.uk
**Phone:** 01924 870508

**Stanningley**
**Ground:** The Arthur Miller Ground, Coal Hill Drive, Leeds LS13 1PA
**Website:** www.stanningleyrugby.co.uk
**E-mail:** stanningleyrugby@aol.com
**Phone:** 0113 256 0847

**Thatto Heath Crusaders**
**Ground:** Hattons Solicitors 'Crusader Park', Close Street, Thatto Heath, St Helens, Merseyside WA9 5JA
**Website:** www.thattoheathcrusaders.org
**E-mail:** info@thattoheathcrusaders.org
**Phone:** 01744 818027

**Underbank Rangers**
**Ground:** The Cross Grounds, Dunford Road, Holmfirth HD9 2RR
**Website:** www.pitchero.com/clubs/underbankrangers
**E-mail:** janetb@hotmail.co.uk
**Phone:** 01484 686744

**Waterhead**
**Ground:** Waterhead Park, Peach Road, Oldham OL4 2HX
**Website:** www.pitchero.com/clubs/waterheadrugbyarlfc
**E-mail:**
**Phone:** 0161 624 9312

**Wath Brow Hornets**
**Ground:** The Clubhouse, Wath Brow, Cleator, Cumbria CA23 3EW
**Website:** www.pitchero.com/clubs/wathbrowhornetsa
**E-mail:** wathbrowhornets@btconnect.com
**Phone:** 01946 811 101

**West Hull**
**Ground:** West Hull Community Park, North Road, Hull HU4 6LQ
**Website:** www.pitchero.com/clubs/westhull
**E-mail:** fiona@everson.com
**Phone:** 01482 502609

**Widnes West Bank**
**Ground:** Ted Gleave Sports Ground, Hutchinson Street, Widnes WA8 0PZ
**Website:** www.wesbankbears.com
**E-mail:** paulfarrell@talktalk.net
**Phone:** 0151 257 7949

**Wigan St Patricks**
**Ground:** Clarington Park, Harper Street, Ince, Wigan WN1 3BN
**Website:** www.pitchero.com/clubs/wiganstpatricksarlfc
**E-mail:** wiganstpatricksarlfc@hotmail.co.uk
**Phone:** 01942 495071

**Woolston Rovers Wizards**
**Ground:** Monks Sports Club, Hillock Lane, Woolston, Warrington WA1 4NF
**Website:** www.pitchero.com/clubs/woolstonroversrlfc
**E-mail:** admin@woolstonrovers.co.uk
**Phone:** 01925 850519

**Wigan St Jude's**
**Ground:** Parsons Meadow, Keats Avenue, Poolstock, Wigan WN3 5UB
**Website:** www.wiganstjudesarlfc.com
**E-mail:** wiganstjudes@talktalk.net
**Phone:** 01942 826808

**York Acorn**
**Ground:** Acorn Sports & Social Club, Thanet Road, Acomb, York YO24 2NW
**Website:** www.yorkacorn.co.uk
**E-mail:**
**Phone:** 01904 330351

# 5. Conference League South

**Bristol Sonics**
**Stadium:** Clifton RFC, Station Road, Cribbs Causeway, Bristol BS10 7TT
Sat nav: BS10 7TB
**Website:** www.bristolsonics.com
**E-mail:** Addresses on the club website

**Leicester Storm**
**Stadium:** New College, Glenfield Road, Leicester LE3 6RN
**Website:** www.pitchero.com/clubs/leicesterstormrlc
**Twitter:** @LeicesterStorm
**Phone:** 07812060687

**Northampton Demons**
**Stadium:** Duston Sports Centre, Cotswold Avenue, Duston, Northampton NN5 6DP
**Website:** www.northamptonrl.co.uk
**E-mail:** patrickwilson@northamptonrl.co.uk
**Phone:** Various phone numbers on the club website.

**Nottingham Outlaws**
**Stadium:** Harvey Hadden Stadium, Wigman Road, Bilborough, Nottingham NG8 4PB
**Website:** www.nottinghamrl.co.uk
**E-mail:** info@nottinghamrl.co.uk
**Phone:** 0115 9553387

**St Albans Centurions**
**Stadium:** The Sports Ground, Toulmin Drive, St Albans, Herts AL3 6DR
**Clubhouse:** 2 High Oaks, New Greens, St Albans, AL3 6DL
**Website:** www.pitchero.com/clubs/stalbanscenturionsrugbyleagueclub
**E-mail:** tonybotts@yahoo.co.uk
**Phone:** 07876-143566

**Sheffield Hallam Eagles**
**Stadium:** Don Valley Stadium. Planned to play at Graham Solley Centre at Bawtry Road when it opens in September 2013.
**Website:** Information on the Sheffield Eagles website, or Sheffield Hallam University: www.shu.ac.uk

# 6. Armed Services grounds

Combined Services Rugby League (CRSL) was established in 1997 after the official recognition of Rugby League by the three Armed Services. CRSL is the highest representative level within the three services and is the coordinating group for representative level in the Royal Navy, Army and Royal Air Force Rugby League Associations.
Each Service organises its own competition at local, unit and corps level. Players are selected for the Service representative teams to play in an annual Inter-Services Competition, which is usually held in September. The best players are selected to represent the Combined Services.

The grounds listed below are the usual venues for home Challenge Cup and inter-service matches. However, it is strongly recommended to check on the service website before travelling to any game.

## Army

**Stadium:** Aldershot Rugby Stadium, Queens Avenue, Aldershot, Hampshire GU11 2JL
**Website:** www.pitchero.com/clubs/armyrugbyleague
**Twitter:** @ArmyRugbyLeague
**History:** This venue was first used for Army Rugby League in 1998, but has been the permanent home only since 2007. Previous grounds used include the Chatham Garrison Stadium and Richmond RFC. The stadium was built for use by both rugby codes. There is a bar / clubroom attached, a covered stand and other refreshment facilities are usually provided. Nearby parking is available. The pitch has floodlights.

## Royal Air Force

**Stadium:** Sultan Qaboos Pavilion, RAF College Cranwell, Lincs NG34 8HB
**Website:** www.raf.mod.uk/rafrugbyleague
**History:** RAF Cranwell's Sultan Qaboos Pavilion has been the home of RAF Rugby League since 2009. It replaced RAF Uxbridge. There is nearby parking, a pavilion with a bar and refreshment facilities, and a temporary covered stand. There are no floodlights.

## Royal Navy

**Stadium:** US Sports Ground, Burnaby Road, Portsmouth, Hants PO1 2EJ
**Website:** www.pitchero.com/clubs/royalnavyrugbyleague
**Twitter:** @RoyalNavyRL
**History:** Burnaby Road was first used by Royal Navy Rugby League in 1999 with two games against the Army.
It replaced HMS Collingwood which staged the inaugural Royal Navy Rugby League game against the RAF in 1998.

## Armed Services grounds

RAF versus The Army at RAF College Cranwell, September 2012, showing the Sultan Qaboos Pavilion in the background.

The Army versus Royal Navy at Aldershot Rugby Stadium in September 2010. The teams come onto the pitch for the development match, with the main stand in the background.

# 7. National Rugby League

**Brisbane Broncos**
**Stadium:** Suncorp Stadium, 40 Castlemaine Street, Milton, Queensland.
**Capacity:** 52,500
**Website:** www.broncos.com.au
**E-mail:** info@broncos.com.au
**Postal address** Locked Bag 10004, Kelvin Grove DC, Queensland 4059
**Phone:** (07) 3858 9111
**Fax:** (07) 3858 9112

**Canberra Raiders**
**Stadium:** Canberra Stadium, ActewAGL Park, 2 Eade Street, Bruce, ACT 2617
**Capacity:** 25,011
**Website:** www.raiders.com.au
**E-mail:** reception@raiders.co.au
**Postal address:** PO Box 3315, Belconnen Business Centre, ACT 2617
**Phone:** (02) 6253 3515
**Fax:** (02) 6253 3546

**Canterbury-Bankstown Bulldogs**
**Stadium:** ANZ Stadium (Stadium Australia), Sydney Olympic Park, NSW 2122
**Capacity:** 83,500
**Website:** www.bulldogs.com.au
**E-mail:** info@bulldogs.com.au
**Office address:** Edison Lane, Belmore, NSW 2192
**Phone:** (02) 9789 8000
**Fax:** (02) 9789 8001

**Cronulla-Sutherland Sharks**
**Stadium:** Toyota Stadium, Woolooware, NSW
**Capacity:** 22,000
**Website:** www.sharks.com.au
**E-mail:** sharks@sharks.com.au
**Postal address:** PO Box 2219, Taren Point, NSW 2229
**Phone:** (02) 9527 8261

**Gold Coast Titans**
**Stadium:** Skilled Park, Centreline Place, Robina, Queensland 4226
**Capacity:** 27,400
**Website:** www.titans.com.au
**E-mail:** info@titans.com.au
**Office address:** 2 Promethean Way, Robina, Queensland 4226
**Phone:** (07) 5656 5650
**Fax:** (07) 5656 5699

**Manly Sea Eagles**
**Stadium:** Brookvale Oval, Pittwater Road, Brookvale 2100, NSW
**Capacity:** 23,000
**Website:** www.seaeagles.com.au
**E-mail:** info@seaeagles.com.au
**Office address:** Sydney Academy of Sport, Wakehurst Parkway, Narrabeen, NSW 2101
**Phone:** (02) 9970 3000
**Fax:** (02) 9972 4022

**Melbourne Storm**
**Stadium:** AAMI Park, Edwin Flack Field, Olympic Boulevard, Melbourne, Victoria 3001
**Capacity:** 30,500
**Website:** www.melbournestorm.com.au
**E-mail:** info@melbournestorm.com.au
**Office address** Melbourne Storm Rugby League Club, AAMI Park, 60 Olympic Boulevard, Melbourne, Victoria 3001
**Phone:** (03) 8412 4900
**Fax:** (03) 8412 4999

**Newcastle Knights**
**Stadium:** Hunter Stadium (Newcastle International Sports Centre), New Lambton, Newcastle, NSW
**Capacity:** 33,000
**Website:** www.newcastleknights.com.au

**New Zealand (VodoPhone) Warriors**
**Stadium:** Mount Smart Stadium, 2 Beasley Avenue, Penrose 1061, Auckland, New Zealand
**Capacity:** 30,000
**Website:** www.warriors.co.nz
**E-mail:** reception@warriors.co.nz
**Postal address:** PO Box 12-224, Penrose 1642, Auckland, New Zealand
**Phone:** (64) 9 526 8822
**Fax:** (64) 9 526 4992

**North Queensland Cowboys**
**Stadium:** Dairy Farmers Stadium, Golf Links Drive, Kirwan, Queensland, 4817
**Capacity:** 26,500
**Website:** www.cowboys.co.au
**E-mail:** cowboys@cowboys.com.au
**Postal address:** PO Box 577, Thuringowa Central, Qld 4817
**Phone:** 1300 (GO COWBOYS) (1300 462 692)
**Fax:** 07 4723 2595

**Parramatta Eels**
**Stadium:** Parramatta Stadium, O'Connell Street, Parramatta 2150, NSW
**Capacity:** 21,487
**Website:** www.parraeels
**E-mail:** eelsreception@parraeels.com.au
**Office address:** 2 Eels Place, Parramatta, NSW 2150
**Phone:** (612) 8843 0300
**Fax:** (612) 8843 0318

**Penrith Panthers**
**Stadium:** Penrith Stadium (Centrebet Stadium, Penrith), Cnr Mulgoa Road & Ransley Street, Penrith NSW 2750
**Capacity:** 22,500
**Website:** www.penrithpanthers.com.au
**E-mail:** rugbyleague@panthers.co.au
**Postal address:** Locked Bag 322, Penrith, NSW 2751
**Phone:** (61)2 4725 6400
**Fax:** (61) 2 4725 6427

**South Sydney Rabbitohs**
**Stadium:** ANZ Stadium (Stadium Australia), Edwin Flack Avenue, Sydney Olympic Park, NSW 2127
**Capacity:** 83,500
**Website:** www.rabbitohs.com
**E-mail:** thumper@rabbitohs.com.au
**Office address:** Level 4, 265 Chalmers Street, Redfern, NSW
**Phone:** (02) 8306 9900
**Fax:** (02) 8306 9911

**St George Illawarra Dragons**
**Stadium (1):** WIN Jubilee Oval, Carlton, NSW
**Capacity:** 22,000
**Stadium (2):** WIN Stadium (Woollongong Showground), Woollongong, NSW.
**Capacity:** 23,750
**Website:** www.dragons.com
**E-mail:** hothothot@dragons.com.au
**Postal address** (Kogarah): Level 1, St George Leagues Club, 124 Princes Hwy, Kogarah NSW 2217
**Phone:** (02) 9587 1966
**Postal address** (Wollongong): Level 1, Steelers Club, Cnr of Harbour & Burelli Streets, Wollongong, NSW 2500
**Phone:** (020) 4225 8299

**Sydney Roosters**
**Stadium:** Allianz Stadium (formerly The Sydney Football stadium), Moore Park, Sydney, NSW 2001
**Capacity:** 45,500
**Website:** www.roosters.co.au
**E-mail:** receptionfootball@sydneyroosters.co.au
**Postal address:** PO Box 693, Paddington, NSW 2021
**Phone:** (02) 8063 3800
**Fax:** (02) 8063 3810

**Wests Tigers**
**Stadium (1):** Allianz Stadium, Moore Park, Sydney, NSW.
**Capacity:** 45,500
**Stadium (2):** Campbelltown Stadium, Pembroke Road, Campbelltown, NSW
**Capacity:** 20,000
**Stadium (3):** Leichhardt Oval, Mary Street, Leichhardt Oval, NSW
**Capacity:** 22,000
**Website:** www.weststigers.com.au
**E-mail:** Website:@weststigers.com.au
**Postal address:** PO Box 169, North Strathfield, NSW 2137
**Street address:** Concord Oval, Loftus Street, Concord NSW 2137
**Phone:** (02) 8741 3300
**Fax:** (02) 9715 6574

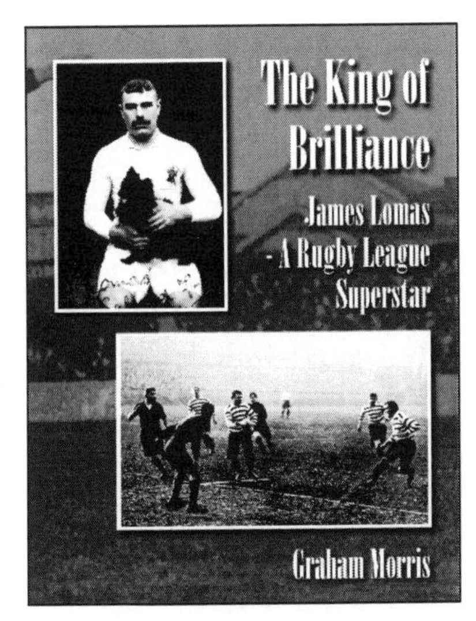


Great new book about one of the sport's genuine legends. James Lomas played for Bramley, Salford, Oldham and York, and won representative honours for Lancashire, Cumberland, England and Great Britain. He captained the first Lions team to tour Australia and New Zealand in 1910. This is the first biography of him.

Published in October 2011 @ £16.95 (hardback). Available for £13.00direct from London League Publications Ltd, PO Box 65784, London NW2 9NS (cheques payable to London League Publications Ltd); credit card orders via our website: www.llpshop.co.uk or from any bookshop @ £16.95.

## *Rugby's Greatest Mystery Who really was F.S. Jackson?*

### A true life rugby detective story

This is the story of a man whose life was made up of mystery, intrigue and deception, but was also a Rugby Union star before the First World War. He played for Leicester and Cornwall when they won the 1908 County Championship. He was selected for the Anglo-Welsh Rugby Union tour to New Zealand and Australia in 1908. However, the RFU recalled him from the tour and banned him from the sport over allegations that he was a professional player, and had played for Swinton in the Northern Union. The scandal around his suspension from rugby union caused great problems for the RFU and almost saw a further split in the game.

He then played Rugby League for New Zealand, against the British Lions in 1910. After the First World War he was reinstated by the New Zealand RU, became an East Coast selector and saw his son play for the All Blacks. For around 60 years he used the name Frederick Stanley Jackson, even though it was not his given name. When he died in 1957 he took to the grave his true identity. Even his family knew little about his early years in England, or even where he came from. **It was a mystery that remained unresolved until now.** The book also includes the development of Leicester Tigers RFC up to the First World War.

Published in March 2012 at £12.95. Available from London League Publications Ltd, PO Box 65784, London NW2 9NS (cheques payable to London League Publications Ltd); credit card orders via www.llpshop.co.uk or from any bookshop.

# Best in the Northern Union

**The pioneering 1910 Rugby League Lions tour of Australia and New Zealand**

**Tom Mather**